CW00545039

MONEY IN THE TWENTY-FIRST CENTURY

The publisher gratefully acknowledges the generous support of the Chairman's Circle of the University of California Press Foundation, whose members are:

Elizabeth Birka-White
Suzanne Holliday Calpestri
Susan McClatchy

MONEY IN THE TWENTY-FIRST CENTURY

Cheap, Mobile, and Digital

RICHARD HOLDEN

UNIVERSITY OF CALIFORNIA PRESS

University of California Press
Oakland, California

© 2024 by Richard Holden

Library of Congress Cataloging-in-Publication Data

Names: Holden, Richard T., author.
Title: Money in the twenty-first century : cheap, mobile, and digital /
    Richard Holden.
Description: [Oakland, California]: University of California Press, [2023] |
    Includes bibliographical references and index.
Identifiers: LCCN 2023020747 (print) | LCCN 2023020748 (ebook) |
    ISBN 9780520395268 (cloth) | ISBN 9780520395275 (ebook)
Subjects: LCSH: Money—21st century.
Classification: LCC HG221 .H76 2023 (print) | LCC HG221 (ebook) |
    DDC 332.409/05—dc23/eng/20230503
LC record available at https://lccn.loc.gov/2023020747
LC ebook record available at https://lccn.loc.gov/2023020748

Manufactured in the United States of America

32 31 30 29 28 27 26 25 24
10 9 8 7 6 5 4 3 2 1

For Hartley and Isobel

Contents

Prologue

IN THE SUMMER OF 2021, US Treasury Secretary Janet Yellen sat down for breakfast with Jay Powell, her successor as chair of the Federal Reserve. It was a weekly ritual that Yellen knew well.

Her office in the Treasury building at 1500 Pennsylvania Avenue was a study in contrasts. Eighteenth-century portraits and deep mahogany woodwork offered a reminder of the past; a Bloomberg terminal and Herman Miller desk chair signified the present. It was a fitting backdrop for the central topic of the meeting: should the US government give its blessing to a private cryptocurrency developed by Facebook?

Powell was in favor. If there was going to be a private, global cryptocurrency, then it would be better for it to be controlled by an American company like Facebook. That way the US government could play a role in establishing the rules of the game. In any case, Facebook just wanted the go-ahead for a trial of diem, as it called its currency. What harm was there in that?

Possibly quite a lot, in Yellen's view. Although she had been in government for nearly two decades—as president of the San Francisco Federal Reserve, then deputy Fed chair, chair, and now as treasury secretary—she was an economics professor at heart. And the economist in her foresaw all kinds of problems.

First, digital currencies involve *network externalities*: the greater the number of people who used diem, the more attractive it would be for other consumers to adopt it. This phenomenon leads to winner-take-all markets in which one firm ends up with a huge market share, like Google in search, Uber in ridesharing, and Amazon in retailing—and, not incidentally, Facebook in social networks. Was this really just a trial for diem, or the first step on a march to market dominance?

Second, would Facebook really control the digital currency? The premise of the blockchains on which digital currencies like bitcoin are built is that they are decentralized and anonymous. This was why a surprisingly large number of frozen-yoghurt shops in New Hampshire accepted bitcoin and other digital currencies like ether. The digital currency movement was born in 2008 out of a distrust of centralized authority in general and government in particular.

Third, cryptocurrencies might have virtues, but they also came with vices—or at least facilitated them. Tax evasion, money laundering, and the arms and illicit drugs trades were already lubricated by cryptocurrency.

For Yellen the downsides of a Facebook digital currency were too great and the benefits too hard to see. But, in professorial style, she wanted to reflect. She told Powell she would get back to him. For Powell's part, although he could approve this trial himself, he wanted Yellen's support in a potentially risky decision. Though Yellen was relatively centrist, she had a lot of political capital with the progressive wing of the Democratic Party as well as with President Joe Biden.

After weeks of reflection, Yellen gave Powell her view. It was his call, she acknowledged, but she couldn't provide her endorsement—and hence political cover—for the Facebook proposal. If he wanted to back the trial, he would have to do it alone. That was the day that diem died.

But digital currencies are still very much alive. The central banks of more than fifty nations are exploring their own digital currencies, or govcoins. China has introduced the e-CNY (the electronic yuan) to 260 million people. The European Union has stated the goal of having a virtual euro by 2025. And the British and US governments are planning their own digital currencies.

Meanwhile other digital currencies, including bitcoin and ether, are worth roughly $2 trillion in total. In March 2022 *Time* magazine dedicated an entire issue to nonfungible tokens (NFTs) and the blockchain, with Vitalik Buterin. the twenty-year-old cofounder of Ethereum, on the cover. In fact, it is the wiry, brilliant, hard-blogging Buterin who is the central figure in the world of private digital currencies and the closest thing that a movement based on decentralization can have to a leader.

For the first time in centuries, there is a rivalry between private and public currencies. And for the first time in history, private currencies might actually win. Even if they don't, the contours of the battle will shape what government currency is and what it can do.

This is also an era of cheap money and mobile money. Official interest rates since the financial crisis of 2008 have been close to zero across most advanced economies. And despite a serious rise in inflation in 2021 and 2022, we will not see a return to the double-digit interest rates of the 1980s. The global balance between the supply of money and the demand for money has permanently shifted.

Modern money is mobile. Money is on our phones more often than in our pockets. A child born in America today will never write a personal check. It's likely that none of us will be handling banknotes by the time that child is old enough to vote. After advocating for a move to a cashless Australia in January 2017, I went an entire year without using cash just to prove a point (and win a bet). And it wasn't even hard.

The world of electronic payments is convenient, but it has a catch. Cash is—or at least can be—anonymous. Mobile money is not. Every transaction using a credit card, debit card, Apple Pay, or other online payment system is recorded. Transactions can be used by tax authorities to identify illegal activity. The anonymity of cash underpins illicit activity ranging from tax evasion to human trafficking. The black economy that cash facilitates is huge. In India it is estimated to be as much as 40 percent of all economic activity.[1] It denies governments the tax base required to fund important services, and it allows criminal activity to flourish. This was the motivation for the November 2016 Indian "demonetization" ordered by Prime Minister Narendra Modi, when large-denomination banknotes were withdrawn from circulation. That episode was disastrous for the country's economy, but it was a telling moment. It showed that cash as a medium of exchange—even in a country that relies heavily on it—is declining in importance.

At the time, the person leading India's central bank, the Reserve Bank of India (RBI), was the renowned economist Raghuram Rajan. He was known not only for his academic brilliance but also for his practical mind. After Rajan left the RBI, it emerged that he had warned the government of the problems that would arise from sucking 86 percent of India's currency out of circulation almost overnight. Nine months before Modi's plan went into action, Rajan had told the government that "although there might be long-term benefits, I felt the likely short-term economic costs would outweigh them."[2] India's demonetization is both an example of how not to become a cashless society and also a warning about the inevitability of a cashless society.

It was Rajan who pointed out that the monetary policy enacted by the US Federal Reserve had spillover effects on emerging-market countries like India. In a speech at the Brookings Institution in April 2014,

Rajan observed that "when monetary policy in large countries is extremely and unconventionally accommodative, capital flows into recipient countries tend to increase local leverage."[3] Not only did cheap money create risks of asset bubbles in countries like the United States, but these risks were exported around the world and will endure.

This book shows how the three characteristics of modern money—cheap, digital, and mobile—will affect the global economy in the twenty-first century. And it is the story of three people—Yellen, Buterin, and Rajan—who have shaped, and will continue to shape, those three forces. It is the interwoven and interconnected tale of a woman born in Brooklyn, New York, the year after World War II ended, who became the foremost policymaker of her generation; an economist born in the early 1960s in Bhopal, Madhya Pradesh, who reached the pinnacle of academia while doing a stint at the International Monetary Fund, running the Reserve Bank of India, and trying to triage the fallout from an attempt to abruptly yank 86 percent of the cash in circulation from a fifth of the world's population; and of a Russian-born Canadian phenom who entered the world only in the mid-1990s, and who came up with the idea for what might become the future of the internet when he was still a teenager.

1

THE YEAR THAT
CHANGED EVERYTHING

IN THE FIRST MILLENNIUM BCE, the total size of the world economy hardly budged: it went from $182 billion to $210 billion. In the next five hundred years it doubled to $430 billion. Then it took off. In 1700 world output was more than $640 billion. By 1820 it was $1.2 trillion.[1] Today it is more than one hundred times that.

This exponential increase in what the world produces has had an extraordinary impact on the standard of living of billions of people. The typical explanation for the economic progress since the mid-eighteenth century is technological advances—particularly the transition from hand to machine production of goods that has come to be known as the Industrial Revolution.

That explanation isn't wrong, but it's incomplete. Economic activity relies on two things: production and trade. The ability for a person to trade with other people in their village, their region, their country, and other parts of the world underpins the division of labor. The idea that there are gains from people specializing in specific tasks or types of production dates to around 2,400 years ago in Plato's *Republic*. It was rightly identified as one of the cornerstones of modern economics by Adam Smith in *The Wealth of Nations*. Technological advances make it possible to improve living standards. But the ability for people to trade and specialize in the use of their talents and effort is what turns possibility into reality.[2]

For millennia, the biggest obstacle to economic efficiency was the absence of money—or, to be a little more precise, the absence of fiat currency (a currency backed by the government that issues it). Without a medium of exchange like money, two people wanting to trade with each other would each to have something that the other wanted. This "double coincidence of wants" could be rare. A medium of exchange that circumvents this problem makes voluntary trades possible and leads to a more efficient use of resources.

It's not surprising, then, that money has been around for a long time. The shekel—about one-third of an ounce of silver—became standard currency in Mesopotamia nearly five thousand years ago.[3] The first coins were minted in the fifth or sixth century BCE, although there is historical dispute about who minted them. The new technology spread to Persia after the conquest of Lydia in 546 BCE, and eventually throughout the world.[4]

Over the centuries currencies have come and gone, and the values of different national currencies have fluctuated wildly. Coins were supplemented by paper banknotes beginning with the Ming Dynasty in China in 1375. From 1870 to 1971, the convertibility of currencies into gold—the gold standard—was at the heart of the international monetary system.[5] More recently, some countries have introduced polymer banknotes that make counterfeiting harder, and credit and debit cards have made monetary transactions easier.

Fundamentally, however, very little changed between the Ming Dynasty and the start of the twenty-first century. Governments of one form or another controlled centralized systems of fiat money and the decision about what currency could be used for exchange within their borders.

That pattern was disrupted in 2008 by three seemingly unconnected phenomena that are likely to redefine money, the roles it performs, and who controls it. First, in the initial decade of the twenty-first century we saw that interest rates in advanced economies could remain remarkably low for long periods—perhaps indefinitely. In response to the 2008 financial crisis, official interest rates in advanced economies were slashed to near zero and more or less stayed there until 2022.

The second phenomenon was technological. In 2008 Apple's CEO, Steve Jobs, in a final act of genius, gave birth to the smartphone with the launch of the iPhone 3G. And while that launch event emphasized the convenience of ordering pizzas online, making calls to friends, and carrying around songs and photos in one's pocket, the truly revolutionary aspect was yet to be apparent. To adapt a phrase from Jobs himself when he launched the iPod, it was an entire bank, in your pocket.[6] Powered by the now-ubiquitous smartphone, digital payments with standard fiat currencies have become dramatically more common. In some parts of the world, digital payment volumes outstrip those of cash.

Also in 2008, the idea for the world's first decentralized currency, a "cryptocurrency" called bitcoin, was announced in an obscure white paper. Suddenly, a single clever idea, by a person or group known only as Satoshi Nakamoto, ended government monopolies on money and ushered in an era of decentralized finance.[7]

This book is about those three phenomena: low interest rates, mobile money, and cryptocurrencies. It is about how they interact to change what money does and who controls it. And because money is quite literally the fuel that powers $100 trillion worth of worldwide economic activity every year, this book is about our economic future.

Although "real interest rates"—the cost of money, accounting for inflation—have moved up and down over the last half century, they were never close to zero for an extended period as they have been for the past decade. Money hasn't just become decentralized. It has become costless, rationed only by lenders' expectations of borrowers' ability to repay the principal.

And though money has been somewhat geographically mobile at least since the 1830s and 1840s, when the arrival of the telegraph made it possible to send money by wire transfers, the internet age has dramatically increased that mobility. By the early 2000s, money could move around the world in a flash, although only between banks that were part of the international financial system, controlled by domestic regulators and international agreements such as the Basel Accords. The smartphone opened the door to digital payments that are more convenient and safer than cash, to instantaneous money transfers between individuals, and to a safe and accessible store of value and means of transacting business for some of the poorest people on the planet.

These three phenomena jointly raise one big question: Can central authorities keep control of the monetary system in the digital age?

The remainder of this book seeks to answer that question, and to contemplate what will happen if the answer is "not for long." It explores the various forms of control that are under threat and how those threats can be countered. Can authorities control the asset bubbles and speculation that stem from arbitrarily cheap money? Can they control what money is used for? Can they still levy taxes?

LOW INTEREST RATES

Since the financial crisis of 2008, near-zero—and sometimes negative—interest rates have become commonplace in advanced economies. At first they could be understood as a necessary monetary-policy response to the events of 2008. With the world plunging into recession, central banks took measures that initially looked much like the standard prescription: cut interest rates until the economy recovers, and then gradually raise them again.

But a funny thing happened on the way to economic recovery. Despite an unprecedented amount of money being pumped into the US, European, and other advanced economies, inflation remained stubbornly low. I say *stubbornly* because since the 1980s, central banks in these economies have set targets of a low and stable amount of inflation—generally between 2 and 3 percent. If inflation seems likely to exceed 3 percent, then interest rates are raised to reduce economic activity and inflation. If inflation rates seem to be dropping below the target, then interest rates can be cut to boost economic growth.

By 2013 it was becoming clear that something in the macroeconomic system wasn't working the way it was supposed to. That year, Larry Summers, a former US treasury secretary, used the term *secular stagnation* (which had origins dating to the late 1930s, with *secular* referring to a long period of time) to describe a low-growth, low-inflation, low-interest-rate economy that can achieve strong growth only through financial bubbles like the one in the US housing market between 2003 and 2007.[8]

Secular stagnation arises from an imbalance between saving and investment. Thanks to an increase in the supply money and reduced demand in advanced economies, we have entered an era of lower economic growth, less frequent and severe bouts of inflation, and permanently low interest rates.

On the investment side, demand has decreased because it has become possible to create enormously valuable companies with relatively modest amounts of capital. It is only a slight caricature to say that a $700 billion company like Facebook was created in a dorm room with a $1,500 laptop and a great idea. Even if one factors in the venture-capital money invested in startup companies like Facebook, Google, Uber, and many others, the investment required to create huge and successful companies today is small compared to the capital requirements of large companies of earlier eras, like US Steel, AT&T, and Standard Oil.

On the savings side, billionaires and sovereign wealth funds, combined with aging societies in advanced economies, have increased the supply of money. The huge concentration of wealth among a relatively small number of individuals in recent years has not only created an unprecedented degree of inequality; it has also led to excess savings. Rich people save more than poor people. People with a billion dollars don't spend as much of their income as people living paycheck to paycheck. And as life expectancy has grown, there has been an increased need to save for longer retirements, both privately and through public pensions.

This combination of new technologies and the concentration of wealth have led to a fundamental structural change in the economy. The laws of supply and demand don't determine only the price of goods, like food or motor vehicles; they also determine the real price of money—or what economists call the *natural rate of interest*. This is the interest rate at which the supply of money and the demand for money are matched.

The price of money is determined by the supply of savings available to borrow and the demand for investment capital. The concentration of wealth, combined with the increased savings of aging societies, has pushed interest rates down. The lower capital requirements of new information technology and internet companies have decreased investment demand, also pushing interest rates down.

These forces have been so strong that the natural rate of interest—the real price of money—has become negative. Because central banks cannot easily set official interest rates below zero (or at least not much below zero), there is an imbalance between the natural interest rate and the actual interest rate in the economy. It is this mismatch that causes secular stagnation.

When there is too much saving and not enough investment, economic growth is weak. One way in which investment demand can rise enough to raise the natural interest rate above zero is through asset bubbles. When lax lending standards, irrational exuberance, and outright fraud led to a huge increase in demand for housing loans in the United States in the first years of this century, economic growth once again appeared strong. But when the housing bubble burst, not only did it plunge most of the world into a severe recession, it also reduced demand for mortgages and hence investment. Central banks had no alternative but to cut interest rates to near zero.

Very low interest rates make it easy for asset price bubbles to form again. We are consigned to a world in which either economic growth is low or it is sustained only by people taking unwise, and sometimes illegal, risks with their own or other people's money.

The economic fallout from the coronavirus pandemic has only compounded this problem. Against a backdrop of unprecedented government spending and significant disruptions to supply chains during the pandemic, inflation in many advanced economies hit levels not seen for decades. In response, central banks around the world began to raise interest rates in late 2021 and early 2022 to keep inflation under control.

While this approach makes good sense in dealing with inflation, higher interest rates make saving more attractive and investing more expensive. And even with this increase, interest rates are likely to return to comparatively low levels, rather than to zero. Moreover, after accounting for inflation, the real cost of borrowing is still negative.

CRYPTOCURRENCIES

In the wake of the 2008–9 financial crisis—a crisis triggered by excessive financial innovation in the form of collateralized debt obligations—an entirely new financial innovation emerged. In 2009 the world's first cryptocurrency, bitcoin, was created. This invention has heralded a new era of private currencies, the expansion of distributed-ledger technology (DLT) or *blockchain*, and the first genuine threat to government monopolies over money since the widespread adoption of fiat currency in the eighteenth century.

Blockchain is a way to witness transactions. Conventionally, transactions have been witnessed by having parties to a transaction write its key elements into a contract and have that contract interpreted by an independent third party, like a court of law. We can think of a contract as a series of statements made by the parties: you will do this, and I will do that; if this happens, then that happens, and so on.

DLT uses a different approach to witnessing the statements. It takes advantage of so-called cryptographic algorithms that are mediated by a computer network. Although DLT has quite a few moving parts, the design is ingenious. And it does something that was previously not thought possible: it allows a decentralized group of people who don't know each other and are acting purely in their own self-interest to, collectively, create trust. By doing so it completely supersedes the need for a centralized authority to witness transactions.

This is a revolution—or at least it could be. If decentralized cryptocurrencies end up supplanting nationally controlled currencies as the dominant means of exchange, then one of the most important powers of the state—the ability to facilitate and regulate commerce—will be seriously undermined.

And this revolutionary aspect of cryptocurrencies is at the heart of why some libertarians were early adopters and vocal advocates of them. For instance, the sleepy New Hampshire town of Keene (population twenty-three thousand) is home to the Free Keene movement, which opposes state power in every guise. Not only are taxes bad, but so are police, and even parking meters and the parking inspectors who monitor compliance, thereby generating revenue for the government. Keene is also the birthplace of the Shire Free Church, whose unlikely mission is weaning its parishioners and their community off government assistance. *New York* magazine justifiably described Keene as "the per capita crypto mecca of the country." It is a town where frozen-yoghurt stores accept bitcoin, where the merits of various different cryptocurrencies are hotly debated, and where the Bitcoin Embassy peddles crypto-themed T-shirts, programming manuals, and books about Austrian economics.[9]

How Blockchain Works

Blockchains that underpin cryptocurrencies like bitcoin or ether are networks of *nodes*, or computers on a network. When two parties (A and B, say) decide to transact, each announces a statement of this intention to the network. The network enables the nodes to observe the two parties' messages and then, crucially, produce evidence that they have heard them. This process, known as *validating* the messages, requires different computers on the network racing to solve cryptographic problems, a process known as *proof of work*.[10]

The cryptographic problems involve a type of one-way mathematical function known as a *hash function*. In a one-way function, if you know the inputs, you can produce the outputs; but if you know only the outputs, you cannot determine the inputs with certainty. Solving such problems, which have become more complex over time, requires specialized computers and large amounts of energy.

When a node on the network observes messages from A and B, the node transforms each message into a "hash." People who observe the hash know that the nodes must have witnessed A making a statement like "I will rent you this apartment for a month," and B saying, "I will pay you one coin for that."

The nature of a hash function means that the node cannot produce the hash unless it has observed the statements of both A and B. In this sense, the hash validates that the overall rental transaction between A and B was announced. When the hash is announced, the network adds it to the list of previously witnessed transactions. The complete list of all such transactions is called the *blockchain*. Because the blockchain is a list of transactions, it is also called a *ledger*. Because that ledger is held by all the nodes on the network, rather than by a single central authority, it is known as a *distributed ledger*.

What Blockchain Means

The existence of cryptocurrencies has significant implications for the balance of power between the state and the individual. Cryptocurrencies have not only threatened government monopolies over money; they have also provided a new catalyst for illicit activity and made it harder for governments to prevent tax evasion. They have the potential to threaten central bank control over monetary policy. In the United States, cryptocurrencies are one of the most pressing concerns for the Treasury, the Federal Reserve, and the Department of Justice.

Moreover, digital currencies are a classic example of a market with *network externalities*. That is, the greater the number of consumers participating in a market, the more attractive it becomes. This virtuous circle is a feature of many digital markets. It leads to "winner-take-most" outcomes in which a dominant player has an extremely high market share. Examples include platforms such as Uber, Facebook, and Amazon; services where machine learning leads to product innovation, such as internet search (Google) or music (Apple Music or Spotify); and hardware underpinned by ecosystem-specific apps (Apple's and Google's phones and app stores).

Network externalities are likely to lead to the dominance of one or a small number of cryptocurrencies. And in that simple fact lies a paradox. A new technology that allows decentralized verification of transactions threatens the monopoly that the state has over money but potentially creates a private monopoly. Even though no individual is ever likely to control bitcoin, ether, or algo, it is entirely possible— some might say it has already happened—that a very small number of currencies, perhaps just two, will dominate the cryptocurrency market.

There is one crucial difference between cryptocurrencies and certain large tech firms: their share structure. Founder's shares in Facebook, for instance, effectively give Mark Zuckerberg perpetual control over the voting rights of the company and hence the major decisions that are made. It is hard to image any individual or concentrated group gaining more than 50 percent of a network's hash rate—which would give them the unfettered ability to rewrite all transactions on a blockchain.

MOBILE MONEY

A form of digital financial transaction more familiar than cryptocurrencies to many people is online payment using platforms such as Apple Pay and Google Pay. The widespread penetration of smartphones and wearable devices, combined with digital payment systems, has led to more digital and fewer cash transactions. Remarkably, these are at least as widely used in many developing countries as in advanced economies. Especially in sub-Saharan Africa, mobile money has displaced cash and the traditional banking system because of the inefficient and insecure nature of that system. High-quality evidence from randomized controlled trials in Kenya and Afghanistan shows that mobile money has decreased poverty, increased female participation in the nonagricultural sector, and increased savings rates.[11]

The cashless society is becoming a reality. Sweden—the first country to issue banknotes, in 1661—has almost completely phased out cash. Other countries with sophisticated payment systems—like Australia— could easily do the same. Going cashless has the potential not only to increase efficiency by cutting down on cash handling and insurance but also to greatly reduce tax evasion in the black economy. In the US, eliminating cash could lead to the collection of more than $100 billion a year in lost tax revenue.[12]

THE CHALLENGE

All of these developments have the potential to do enormous harm or to create significant good. The challenge facing governments is how to harness these innovations without killing them. I argue that governments of advanced economies should create their own digital currencies—like a digital US dollar, digital pound, and digital euro—before a global private currency, powered by network externalities, emerges as dominant. This is a pressing concern. Although Facebook failed in its attempts to institute digital currencies (libra and diem), Amazon, Apple, and Google could all pursue similar strategies if they chose to.

The rising levels of US government debt, combined with the growth of China into the world's largest economy, have suddenly raised the prospect of the US dollar's losing its status as the global reserve currency—the currency most widely held by central banks and monetary authorities of other countries. That would lead to the US government's losing the low borrowing rates and seemingly unlimited power to issue bonds—the so-called exorbitant privilege—that goes with it.

In what follows I paint a picture of the future of money in the digital age and provide a road map for governments to preserve their role in the creation, management, and regulation of money—and the economic activity that goes with it.

Through the creation of a central bank digital currency—I call it *fedcoin*—the United States government could facilitate the smart contracting revolution known as Web3. Fedcoin should use a centralized ledger, run by the Federal Reserve, rather than a distributed ledger or blockchain as cryptocurrencies do. This approach has several advantages. First, it is more secure. Second, it uses energy and computational resources more efficiently. Third, it can suppress activities like dealing in illicit goods or human trafficking while preserving substantive personal privacy and anonymity in contracting. Fedcoin would protect the United States against a Chinese central bank digital currency that could displace the US dollar as the global reserve currency and against a private digital currency in the mold of Facebook's libra that could threaten monetary sovereignty and the US tax base.

Blockchain technology emerged out of a profound distrust of centralized authority, emanating from the 2008 financial crisis. But the main innovations it promises—the introduction of digital money and Web3—are applicable to a central bank digital currency. Giving up on the distributed ledger would advance the technological promise of an official digital currency.

Decentralized trust—and hence blockchain technology—will remain crucial for smart contracts and Web3. But the currency that powers these contracts can, and should, be run on a centralized ledger, which, in my vision, resides with the Federal Reserve.

The fedcoin proposal raises a number of complex questions. What would be the impact on the monetary sovereignty of other advanced economies? How could privacy concerns be addressed? What would be the impact on commercial banks? Could the US successfully transition to the new monetary policy regime that fedcoin would necessitate? This book is neither the first nor the last word on these questions, but I hope it provides a useful framework in which to discuss them.

I start by looking at a single transaction. From this pebble thrown into the water, I follow the expanding ripples. I examine the infrastructure that permits that transaction, the currencies that underpin it, the race for control of those currencies, the impact on monetary policy, the international monetary system, and finally the impact of money on politics in the digital age.

Chapter 2 describes how a cashless society will work and why it is inevitable, even in a world with natural disasters that can take down power grids. It discusses how governments can and should aid the rapid transition to a fully cashless economy.

Chapter 3 discusses how the monetary and fiscal systems fit together, how money is created, and why inflation occurs. It then shifts focus to digital payments, such as those made using tap cards, mobile devices, and digital bank accounts. It describes the convenience and security of these technologies in advanced economies and the enormous social good they have done and will continue to do in developing economies.

Chapter 4 turns to digital currencies and explains the features of cryptocurrencies powered by blockchain technology from a practical perspective. Chapter 5 then discusses the race for supremacy in digital currencies between private issuers and governments, explaining why it is imperative that governments win this race.

Chapter 6 explores the competition among the United States, China, and other countries to position their national currency as the global reserve—the safest store of value—and the implications of digital money in this contest.

Chapter 7 looks at the price rather than the nature of money. It discusses the reasons that interest rates fell so much after the 2008 financial crisis, why they have stayed low for so long, and why they will likely remain relatively low in advanced economies. This chapter also stresses that although the present and future of money is digital, governments cannot simply create money, as has been advocated by proponents of modern monetary theory (MMT), without attention to the consequences. This chapter explains why governments will always need to attend to national debt and fiscal capacity, even in the era of fully digital money.

Chapter 8 concludes with some observations about the implications of digital currency for politics and future technological developments.

2

THE CASHLESS SOCIETY

IF ANYONE WAS BORN to be a central banker, it was Raghuram Rajan. After receiving an engineering degree from the Indian Institute of Technology in 1985 and an MBA from the India Institute of Management two years later, he embarked on a PhD at the Massachusetts Institute of Technology (MIT). After receiving tenure from the University of Chicago Booth School of Business just four years after completing his PhD and winning the inaugural Fischer Black Prize for the best financial economist under forty, Rajan served as chief economist of the International Monetary Fund (IMF) from 2003 to 2007. After several years back in Chicago, he returned to public service as the chief economic adviser to the Indian government in 2012, and in 2013 was appointed governor of the Reserve Bank of India (RBI).

Rajan's signature accomplishment during his term at the RBI was to chart a path to conquering inflation and making monetary policy more independent of government. This was the great accomplishment of the Volcker era in the United States and the inflation-targeting approach that was pioneered by the Reserve Bank of New Zealand in 1990 and was adopted in advanced economies around the world. From the beginning of his term, Rajan sought to underscore the RBI's credibility. In a speech in early 2014 he said, "The best way for the central bank to generate growth in the long run is for it to keep inflation low and steady. . . . In order to generate sustainable growth, we have to fight inflation first."[1] It is hard to think of a starker contrast than that between the considered, clear-thinking Rajan and the populist firebrand prime minister, Narendra Modi, who were the two central characters in the ill-fated effort to eliminate the use of cash in India.

Indian demonetization was less about getting rid of cash than it was about replacing allegedly ill-gotten cash with different banknotes. But the episode contains important lessons, because if the world is to go cashless, then it will need to retire the banknotes that billions of people use every day. India's approach is an example of what *not* to do. But before we get to that, it's important to think about what a future without cash will look like, and how close we are to it.

IN A BITING CRITIQUE of his fellow venture capitalists, PayPal cofounder Peter Thiel famously quipped in 2013 that "we wanted flying cars. Instead we got 140 characters." Even if we have had to settle for Twitter, it's worth reflecting on how technology has changed our everyday routines in the past twenty years.

Imagine yourself as an affluent, health-conscious early riser in 2003 with a love of good coffee. After lacing up your Nikes for a run, you might have grabbed your recently released iPod and a pair of wired headphones, and slipped a $5 bill into your pocket for a stop at Starbucks at the end of your run. (Maybe a $10 bill if you wanted to grab a newspaper too.)

Fast-forward to 2023. Your AirPods don't have wires, and your biggest choice is between taking your iPhone or just your Apple Watch. Either way you can tap your device to pay for your caffeine hit. Everything is slicker—almost frictionless. There's no more remembering to stop at an ATM to be sure you have enough cash for the next morning, no more loose change to deal with.

From the point of view of an economist, technology has done something more fundamental than deliver a flying car. It has changed the most basic building block of economic activity: the *transaction*. Exchanging money for a skim latte has become more efficient. Or, to be more precise, the *transaction costs*—the hassle involved in making that exchange happen—have been reduced. To paraphrase Josh Lyman, the deputy chief of staff in the TV series *The West Wing*, "That may not sound like much to you and me, but to an economist that's a week in St. Barts." Here's why.

Making that very simple transaction more efficient reverberates throughout the whole economy. Digital payments make Starbucks faster at processing each customer's order, which enables it to serve more customers with the same number of employees. Starbucks doesn't need to worry about stocking a cash register drawer with enough bills and coins of all denominations in order to make change for its customers. At the end of the day the company saves labor costs because the staff doesn't have to count all the cash, put coins in special wrappers, and deposit the money in their bank's night safe. Less cash means fewer robberies, so the store's insurance costs are lower. They don't have to worry about employee theft. The list goes on.

Following this logic, one might wonder why cash exists at all anymore. If cashless payments are more convenient for both the party making them and the party receiving them, then why don't we have a fully cashless society?

BECOMING CASHLESS

There are three possible answers to the question of why cash still exists. The first is that cashless payments are perhaps not a superior technology, or at least not for everyone. The second is that cashless payments are a superior technology and will win out eventually, but it will take time to wean people and businesses off cash. The third is that better technologies do not necessarily win out in the long run. Perhaps cashless payments are the Betamax of the twenty-first century. As this is a reference that even I am barely old enough to recognize, I will explain it later in this chapter. But first, let's deal with the issue of convenience.

An obvious concern about cashless payments is that they are not as secure as cash. This important but ultimately misplaced concern is addressed in the next chapter, when I discuss the technological aspects of the monetary system. For now, let's just assume that digital payments are at least as safe as cash.

Convenience

To make the case that cashless payments are more convenient than cash, we need a clear idea of what is good, and not so good, about cash. This is the sort of innocuous-seeming question that is easy to articulate and difficult to answer. So I'm simply going to assert a few advantages of cash and some of its drawbacks. Some of these are also characteristics of other mediums of exchange.

GOOD THINGS ABOUT CASH

1. *Cash is a widely accepted medium of exchange.* Essentially all countries have an official currency that is legal tender. That means that shops, restaurants, and other providers of goods or services are legally obligated to accept that currency in

exchange for whatever they are selling. A commonly accepted currency helps reduce the costs of transactions. You don't need to figure out whether cash will be accepted at the restaurant you are planning to go to tonight—or, if it isn't, convert your cash into some other means of payment.

Interestingly, this claim, which was almost universally true just a few years ago, is becoming less true. The coronavirus pandemic led to many shops not wanting to handle cash. If they did not (illegally) refuse to accept cash, many put up signs saying that they preferred electronic payments. And even beggars in Beijing have QR codes and use WeChat Pay.

2. *Cash is portable.* Since cash comes in different denominations—from small-denomination coins to large-denomination banknotes—it is fairly easy to carry around a sufficient amount of cash for most routine transactions and purposes.

3. *Cash is fast.* There's no delay in settling a payment with banknotes or coins. Or more accurately, once the amount has been counted and agreed between the parties—a process that could take some time and depends on the denominations used—the exchange is instantaneous.

4. *Cash is secure.* Unlike digital payments or money stored in bank accounts, cash cannot be hacked. As long as you maintain physical possession of the cash, it's yours.

5. *Cash is anonymous.* With some exceptions for relatively large cash payments, nobody is legally required to record cash transactions. These transactions, their nature, and the parties involved, remain private.

6. *Cash is often a good store of value.* Because cash can be used in the future, it is a means of saving as well as a medium of exchange. As long as inflation is not too high (a big "if" to which I will return shortly), then cash retains its value reasonably well over moderate time frames.

7. *Cash is technology free.* Cash doesn't involve technology or third parties. It functions when the power is out and depends only on the payer being able to present banknotes or coins.

BAD THINGS ABOUT CASH

1. *Cash is not very secure.* Although cash can't be hacked, it can easily be stolen. Now, in a society with good rule of law, people are rarely mugged in broad daylight for small amounts of cash. But not all societies are marked by good rule of law, and even in advanced economies crime is common in certain places and at certain times. Large amounts of cash are especially vulnerable to theft. A person walking away from an ATM with hundreds of dollars in cash—especially late at night—is an obvious target. Seniors or those with limited mobility are particularly at risk. And storing significant sums of cash "under the mattress" exposes one to possible loss from burglary, fire, and other misfortunes.

2. *Cash is anonymous.* The very anonymity that cash provides—and which is valued by many users of it—also facilitates illicit activity of all kinds—from trafficking in drugs to trafficking in people—and tax evasion. These activities can be extremely costly to society. The One study estimated that the shadow economy in thirty-six of the thirty-eight advanced economies of the OECD was equivalent to 16.5 percent of gross domestic product (GDP).[2]

3. *Cash is often not a good store of value.* Cash maintains its value over time only if it can buy the same quantity of goods or services in the future that it can today. Inflation—the increase in prices over time—reduces this value. Because cash doesn't earn any interest, it is a good store of value only if inflation is close to zero. For much of the past thirty years, inflation in advanced economies has been relatively modest—around 2–3

percent a year. But in late 2021—because of fiscal stimulus during the pandemic, the disruption of supply chains, and very low official interest rates—inflation began to approach 10 percent in a number of advanced economies.

In some circumstances, inflation can become so high that it feeds on itself. This phenomenon, known as *hyperinflation*, completely destroys the value of cash. The most infamous example is that of the German mark in the early 1920s. Burdened by large reparations payments imposed by the Treaty of Versailles (which marked the end of World War I), the German government began to simply print money. This led to inflation. By October 1923 German's *monthly* inflation rate was nearly 30,000 percent.[3] So a loaf of bread that cost 250 marks in January 1923 cost 200 million marks by the end of the year. This wasn't the first or the last example of hyperinflation. Similar episodes occurred in Holland in 1634, France in 1795, Zimbabwe in 2006, and Venezuela in 2013 and 2018.[4]

Comparing Cash and Cashless Payments

So cash has a lot of pros and a few cons. How does it compare to cashless payments, such as debit cards, Apple Pay, Google Pay, and cryptocurrencies? These technologies have various features, but for now I'm going to focus on the basic example of a bank account with a debit card attached to it—either a tap card (a physical debit card with a chip that can be read by point-of-sale equipment) or a debit card loaded onto a portable device such as a mobile phone or watch.

Both cash and cashless payment are claims on the same underlying currency—such as the dollar, euro, yen, or peso—and thus are equivalent on some counts. They are affected by inflation in exactly the same ways and so are equivalent as stores of value. In other ways they differ.

In terms of speed they are close to equivalent, but a digital payment is faster at the point of sale than cash because it requires no physical exchange or counting of banknotes and coins. Both cash and digital payment methods are portable, but digital payments offer advantages in portability: you don't have to decide in advance how much you can spend without replenishing your supply, and carrying large amounts of cash is inconvenient.

On security grounds, cash can't be hacked, but it can be physically stolen, whereas digital payments can, in principle, be hacked but can't be physically stolen. Which is the bigger risk? Well, in the United States in 2021 there were thirty-three thousand reported instances of bank fraud—and many of the victims had part or all of their money returned.[5] By contrast, there were more than 4.6 million instances of larceny theft in the United States that year.[6]

Cash is anonymous, and digital payments are not. Thus cash preserves privacy better than cashless payments, but it opens the door to the shadow economy, with its illicit activities and widespread tax evasion. In other words, the only personal convenience that the anonymity of cash provide comes in the sense of not getting caught committing a crime. From a social perspective one can't credit this as a plus in the cash column.

Finally, isn't cash superior when the power is out or the communications networks are down? This is a question that perennially comes up in conversations on talkback radio about a cashless society. The answer is, not really. When the power is out, stores don't want to sell you anything. In fact, it's not safe for them to be open, so they're usually not. Similarly, if the internet is down, most shops (with the exception of some small convenience stores and the like) cannot function because their point-of-sale equipment, even for cash transactions, is inoperable. If cash has an advantage during natural disasters, it's moot, because nobody's trying to buy or sell things during natural disasters. As I put it once to a talkback caller: "If there's a tsunami, you're probably not going out for coffee, right?"

Overall, digital payments are generally equivalent or superior to cash. This assertion comes with one important condition: the spender has to know how to use the digital payment method. For young children or seniors, this may not always be the case.

While smartphones and wearable devices may be exciting to some of us, they are confusing, if not terrifying, to others. They are also not universally accessible. iPhones may be cool, but they're not cheap. So when a seventy- or eighty-year-old is confronted with the end of cash, there may be a completely understandable fear. How will they give their grandkids some cash inside a birthday card? What happens if they don't understand online banking? They like to pay their utility bills by taking cash to the post office—as many people in the United Kingdom do. What's going to happen to that? They may already be concerned that their familiar routine of going into the bank branch has been made more difficult by reduced mobility and the closure of many bank branches.

Similarly, many parents like to give schoolchildren a small amount of cash to be able to buy a treat at school, or go to the shops with their friends. They might not want their kids to be running around with a debit card or a mobile phone with payment features enabled. These legitimate concerns must be addressed in making the transition to a cashless society that doesn't leave anyone behind.

Phasing Out Cash

If cashless payments are superior, but an overnight switch away from cash would create chaos, how does a country phase out cash gradually but deliberately? Thankfully we don't have to theorize about this too much, as some countries have already traveled a long way down this path. The most notable example is Sweden, but there also some important lessons to be learned from other countries, including Australia.

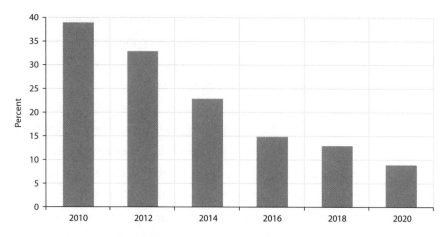

Figure 1. Use of cash in Sweden. *Source*: Bank of Sweden Payments Report, www.riksbank.se
/globalassets/media/rapporter/betalningsrapport/2020/engelsk/payments-report-2022. pdf.

Since 2010, Sweden has introduced new technologies and new infrastructure and made a concerted policy effort to bring the country close
to going cashless. As the Swedish central bank, the Riksbank, has documented, the proportion of people who reported using cash for their
last transaction fell from 39 percent in 2010 to just 9 percent in 2020.

Phasing out cash requires a payment infrastructure that makes cashless payments easy. That includes point-of-sale (POS) equipment that
accepts card payments. The first generation of these machines required
users to swipe the magnetic strip on their card through the machine and
sometimes to enter a personal identification number (PIN). The next
generation of payment systems involved cards with an embedded chip
that was inserted into the POS machine for the chip to be read. Current-
generation POS equipment allows a card to simply be tapped on or near
a machine that reads the chip using near-field communication (NFC).

In addition to tap cards, POS machines equipped with NFC technology can take payments from smartphones (using, for example, Apple
Pay or Google Pay) or wearable devices such as smart watches.

In Sweden, a widely used smartphone app called Swish facilitates
electronic transfers between individuals or to businesses.[7] This allows

people to split bills at a restaurant without having to wait days for a bank transfer to take place or use cash to make side payments to the person who pays the whole bill. Swish was made possible by a consortium of banks banding together to provide a real-time payments system. In a country with a total population of 10.35 million people, there are more than 8 million private users of Swish. In May 2022 they made 80 million Swish payments. Other countries have a similar system that facilities instantaneous payments between individual bank account holders. Australia's is known as the New Payments Platform (NPP), launched in February 2018.[8] All it requires is that a user set up a (free) PayID, which can be a mobile phone number, email address, or other unique identifier that is linked to a bank account. Anyone with a PayID can make an instant payment to anyone else with a PayID.

The tap payments that underpin the move to a cashless Sweden are fast, convenient, and secure. To prevent thieves from "skimming" card data, the two major card networks, Visa and Mastercard, adhere to a standard that requires the customer's card to be within four centimeters (about an inch and a half) of the payment terminal for the transaction to work. A unique security code is generated for each transaction, and the card companies effectively insure their customers against fraud. So cashless payment is secure from the customer's perspective.

But some people still prefer to use cash for certain purchases. Even the Swedish government website that documents and celebrates the move to a cashless society contains the story of Stefan, a seventy-three-year-old who wants to keep using cash, at least for some things. Stefan says: "Especially when I go to Systembolaget [the state monopoly store that sells alcohol]. I never pay by card there, because I don't want the bank to know how much I spend on wine."[9]

This sentiment might seem a little paranoid. Is there really somebody in a bank looking through the top spenders on wine? Almost surely not. And there are a range of privacy and consumer-protection laws in many jurisdictions that would make the use of such information a crime. On the other hand, in some countries there is widespread state surveillance about all manner of activities. And the use of artificial intelligence to predict certain behaviors could, in principle, lead people to want to shield their spending on certain goods or services.

Of course, regardless of state surveillance, some people may want to hide certain purchases from a partner or spouse. Cash is a convenient way of doing this. But it doesn't make for a particularly compelling public defense of cash. As such, it is unlikely to stand in the way of a move to a cashless society.

The issue of privacy is one of rules and norms, not technology. While technology enables surveillance—as China's "social credit" system demonstrates—norms and rules prohibit such surveillance in most liberal democracies.

A more pressing concern is the exclusion of seniors from a cashless society. There is an understandable need for education campaigns to get seniors comfortable with such technology, but those are not a significant barrier.

In countries where effectively all adults have a bank account with a tap-enabled debit card attached, and with NFC point-of-sale equipment and payment platforms such as Swish in Sweden or the NPP in Australia, the path to a cashless society is relatively easy. My three-year plan for Australia to go fully cashless is equally applicable to any country that meets these criteria.[10]

Australia's cash denominations are $100, $50, $20, $10, and $5 bills; and $2, $1, 50-cent, 20-cent, 10-cent, and 5-cent coins. In the first year of a three-year plan to eliminate cash, the government would abolish the $100 bill with a twelve-month notification period. That's ample time for people holding such bills to deposit them at a bank. In Australia, the $100 bill represents about 46 percent of outstanding Australian banknotes. Year 2 would be the retirement year for the $50 bill. That's another 47 percent of the currency gone. In year 3 the government would—almost literally—mop up the small change.

This plan would not work, however, for a society in which many citizens do not have bank accounts. It is estimated that about 5.4 percent of US households are "unbanked."[11] And not all advanced economies have systems with NFC technology at the point of sale and a payments platform that permits instantaneous transfers between accounts.

An additional innovation that would push things along is a central bank digital currency (CBDC) or govcoin (see chapter 5). With a CBDC, with all residents having a bank account, and with a sophisticated payments system in place, there would be little rationale for traditional cash.

Getting Stuck with Inferior Technology?

Even if everyone were to agree that cash is an inferior technology, a cashless society would not be inevitable. This is because the widespread use of a payment method is what economists call a *coordination game*, and there can be multiple equilibria in this game. That is, we might not all opt for the best means of payment.

It is widely acknowledged that Betamax was a superior videotape technology to VHS, but VHS became the dominant standard. At one point—I can vaguely remember it—there were two sections in video rental stores that offered the same movies, one on Beta and the other on VHS. But over time, with more people having VHS machines, video stores tended to hold more VHS movies. As a result, it became more attractive for companies to produce movies on VHS and more attractive for consumers to have a VHS machine to take advantage of the greater range of movies available for rent. It was a self-reinforcing virtuous circle for VHS and a doom loop for Beta. So the inherent superiority of a technology like Betamax or digital payments doesn't guarantee its eventual dominance.

If we all decided to use digital payments, businesses would then want to accept only digital payments, and it would be impossible for anyone to deviate from the process by deciding that they wanted to use cash, since merchants simply wouldn't accept it. But similarly, if merchants accepted only cash, it would be impossible for digital payments to get a foothold. Nobody would invest in the point-of-sale technology that facilitated them, and so we would end up in an all-cash equilibrium.

Since advanced economies are currently in a hybrid situation where cash and digital payment operate side by side, digital payments have obviously gained a foothold. But coordination problems can and do easily arise in these hybrid situations. If some merchants demand cash and can get a sufficient number of customers to continue to use cash, then it won't just fade away. This is the case in plenty of advanced economies at present. To avoid value-added and income tax, certain tradespeople—like plumbers, mechanics, and cleaners—demand to be paid in cash, and lots of customers feel that they have no alternative but to comply. Sure, this is illegal tax evasion, but it's unlikely that authorities are going to invest the resources necessary to catch these relatively small-time operators. If we could prevent this behavior by getting rid of cash, the tax dodgers would be worse off because they would have to pay more tax, but taxpayers would be better off. On top of this, phasing out cash would eliminate all the inefficiencies and costs that come with it: note printing, coin minting, cash handling, insurance, transportation, storage, and other costs.

Economists have understood for some time that although multiple equilibria can exist, there are ways in which we can tip the balance toward the superior equilibrium. An old idea from the Nobel laureate Thomas Schelling is that an equilibrium might be "focal." And it is certainly possible for government policy to make one type of payment focal by making it the primary (or only) form of payment for government services. An even more powerful approach might be for governments to take measures that can help bring about a cashless equilibrium. If government provides infrastructure such as a payment platform backbone, cashless payments can be made more attractive, leading to greater use of cashless payments by both consumers and retailers. A central bank digital currency might be the most powerful coordination device of all.[12]

INDIA'S DEMONETIZATION: A CAUTIONARY TALE

Although I argue that governments should facilitate a transition to a cashless society, there are significant risks involved in moving too fast, or in the wrong way. India's demonetization in 2016 is a cautionary tale. It is important to note that the Indian demonetization was not intended to bring about a transition to a cashless society but rather to deal with corruption and tax evasion facilitated by large-denomination banknotes. There were also serious problems with the execution of the policy. Nevertheless, the episode highlights some of the pitfalls faced by other countries seeking to go cashless.

In India, 90 percent of transactions by value and as many as 98 percent by volume take place in cash, compared to 9 percent in Sweden and around 25 percent in the less-digital United States.[13] In 2016, 86 percent of all Indian cash in circulation was in the form of the two largest-denomination bills, the 500- and 1000-rupee bills. On November 8, 2016, the Indian government announced an immediate ban on these two banknotes. At the same time, Prime Minister Narendra Modi announced that new 500- and 2000-rupee notes would go into circulation on November 10. Until December 30, Indian citizens could go to any bank branch and exchange the old bills for a credit to their bank account. Anyone seeking to convert more than 250,000 rupees (about US $3,500) had to explain why they held that amount of cash. If the explanation was not acceptable to the government, the holder would have to pay a fine.

One reason for the demonetization was commendable. With a massive shadow economy—estimated at somewhere between one-fifth and one-quarter of total output—India had serious difficulties in levying sufficient taxes to provide a social safety net.[14] Tax evasion was surely part of the reason why India's tax-to-GDP ratio in 2016 was around 11 percent, compared to about 25 percent for Australia and 35 percent for Denmark.[15] In addition, corruption undermines investor confidence, leading to less investment and economic growth.

Modi asserted in his speech that "inflation becomes worse through the deployment of cash earned in corrupt ways. The poor have to bear the brunt of this. It has a direct effect on the purchasing power of the poor and the middle class." He also claimed that the move would help counteract terrorism, saying, "Terrorism is a frightening threat. . . . Have you ever thought about how these terrorists get their money? Enemies from across the border run their operations using fake currency notes. . . . Many times, those using fake five hundred and thousand rupee notes have been caught."[16]

The move was roundly criticized by the distinguished Indian economists Kaushik Basu and Nobel laureate Amartya Sen. Not everyone was critical, however. Jagdish Bhagwati, an eminent scholar and Columbia University professor, described the move as "a courageous and substantive economic reform that, despite the significant transition costs, has the potential to generate large future benefits."[17] Yet on balance, it was hard to argue that those "transaction costs"—a lovely euphemism—did not vastly outweigh the benefits. In one poignant example, it was reported that "a child . . . died at a hospital owned by union culture and tourism minister Mahesh Sharma, after the staff refused to accept old notes for treatment."[18] Addressing the wider implications, the *Forbes* writer Wade Shepard pointed out that Modi's demonetization "caused a sudden breakdown in India's commercial ecosystem," and that damage was done across the economy.[19] Sectors that used cash almost exclusively—like agriculture and fishing—were hit especially hard. And the legitimate informal market essentially closed, destroying livelihoods with it. On top of all that, people waited in lines for hours to exchange their expired banknotes, sometimes to no avail.

In retrospect all of this seems predictable. The abruptness with which the policy was announced was intended to prevent those with illicitly obtained cash stockpiles from converting them into other stores of value, like jewelry, but it turned out that most had already done so. That abruptness sucked an enormous amount of money out of the economy, causing a massive breakdown in economic activity. The pace at which new bills became available and could be placed into circulation was always going to be too slow.

Raghuram Rajan had, in fact, seen these problems coming. Early in his term as governor of the reserve bank—but before the government had approached him about demonetization—Rajan was asked about possible demonetization as a means of discouraging illicit activities. He replied:

> Unfortunately, my sense is, the clever find ways around it. Black money hoarders find ways to divide their hoard into many smaller pieces. You find that people who haven't thought of a way to convert black to white, throw it into the hundi in some temples. I think there are ways around demonetization. It is not that easy to flush out the black money. A fair amount of unaccounted cash is typically in the form of gold and therefore even harder to catch. . . . I would focus more on incentives that lead to generation and the retention of black money. There were a lot of incentives on taxes and the current tax rate in the country was for the most part reasonable.[20]

After leaving office, and waiting a year out of deference to the government, Rajan revealed what he had thought about the Modi demonetization plan.

> I was asked by the government in February 2016 for my views on demonetization, which I gave orally. Although there might be long-term benefits, I felt the likely short-term economic costs would outweigh them, and felt there were potentially better alternatives to achieve the main goals. I made these views known in no uncertain terms. I was then asked to

prepare a note, which the RBI put together and handed to the government. It outlined the potential costs and benefits of demonetization, as well as alternatives that could achieve similar aims. If the government, on weighing the pros and cons, still decided to go ahead with demonetization, the note outlined the preparation that would be needed, and the time that preparation would take. The RBI flagged what would happen if preparation was inadequate. The government then set up a committee to consider the issues. The deputy governor in charge of currency attended these meetings. At no point during my term was the RBI asked to make a decision on demonetization.[21]

Even in terms of its original objectives, India's demonetization was largely a failure. Ninety-seven percent of the demonetized notes were turned in, suggesting that money from the shadow economy had effectively been broken up into smaller amounts or held in other stores of value, such as jewelry, property, or gold. While the move might have removed counterfeit notes from circulation, the 97 percent exchange means they were effectively swapped for genuine bills, and counterfeits of the new 2,000-rupee notes soon sprang up.[22] The journalist Wade Shepard, who followed the entire episode closely, summed it up this way: "Curbing the black economy and wiping out counterfeits—two intentions that galvanized the population and bolstered wide support for the initiative—appear to have been complete flops."[23]

In short, the Indian demonetization was an example of what *not* to do in removing cash from the economy. Ironically, although its goal was not to move to a cashless society, the move would have had a far greater chance of succeeding if it had been a move to digital money. But without near-universal banking, and without a sophisticated payments system of the type discussed above, that was never a possibility.

3

MOBILE MONEY AND DIGITAL BANKING

||||||||||||||||||||||||||||||||||||||||||||||||||||||||||||||||||||||||||||||||||||||||||||||||||||||||||||||||||||||||||||||||||||||||||||||

THE ART AND SCIENCE of central banking has evolved over many decades. Giant figures have been at the helm of the US Federal Reserve during that time. Paul Volcker is rightly credited with breaking the back of inflation and giving the Federal Reserve its credibility during his stint as chair from 1979 to 1987. Alan Greenspan, who served five terms as Fed chair from 1987 to 2006, was described by the journalist Bob Woodward as simply "Maestro" in his 2000 book. And Ben Bernanke—a distinguished scholar turned central banker— deserves great credit for steering the United States, and to an extent the global, economy through the 2008 financial crisis during his two terms from 2006 to 2014.

But it is arguably Janet Yellen who has written the modern playbook for central bankers. She is not a six-foot-seven, tough-talking inflation buster like Volcker. She hasn't cultivated a mystique for cryptic communications (or "Fedspeak") like Greenspan. And though she is a great scholar and towering intellect, she isn't primarily a monetary economist or historian of the Great Depression like Bernanke. Yet Yellen was *the* central figure at the Fed for two decades, and she oversaw, refined, and applied all of the modern central banking tools.

It was Yellen who reconciled the two potentially incompatible components of the Fed's dual mandate: achieving stable prices and maximum employment. It was Yellen who introduced the more transparent communication paradigm that is now taken for granted. It was Yellen who first drew serious attention to the housing bubble of the early 2000s. And it was Yellen who, as President Barack Obama remarked when nominating her as Fed chair, "understands the human costs when Americans can't find a job." He went on to say: "She has said before, 'These are not just statistics to me. The toll is simply terrible on the mental and physical health of workers, on their marriages, on their children.' So Janet understands this. And America's workers and their families will have a champion in Janet Yellen."[1]

Yellen's insights are at the heart of the discussion of cheap money, asset bubbles, and government finances in chapter 7. But Yellen is also central to this chapter, because to understand digital banking, we need to understand central banking, how money is created, and how it flows through the economy.

In the previous chapter I focused on individual financial transactions and the transition from cash as the primary medium of exchange to a cashless society with all-digital transactions. Now I turn to the monetary system in which these transactions occur.

THE MONETARY SYSTEM AND INFLATION

At a time when inflation has spiked—something that hasn't happened for most of this century—it is important to understand how prices are affected by the amount of money in existence and the forms in which it exists. One of the crucial functions of money is to act as a store of value, and the degree to which a certain type of money is a good store of value depends on what goods and services it can buy in the future.

Money exists within a system of commercial banks—acting as intermediaries between savers and borrowers—and central banks, operated by national governments, that provide stability to that system and ultimately determine the rate of interest (which is simply the price of money).

Banks

Commercial banks perform three main functions: they pool savings from many savers, they spread the risk of lending across many borrowers, and they solve information problems.

Imagine that you have saved a couple of thousand dollars and you'd like to earn interest on it—at least enough to cover the increase in prices that tends to happen over time (i.e., inflation). To do that, you have to find someone with a more productive use for the money than you have. It might be somebody who really needs to buy a car, fund their education, or buy a house. There are plenty of these folks around, but how do you find them? And if you do find them, you might discover that the $2,000 you're willing to lend out is less than they need to borrow. Banks solve this problem by pooling money from lots of savers and efficiently finding borrowers.

Even if you did find someone who wanted to borrow exactly $2,000, lending it to them would be risky. Even an honest and reliable borrower could lose their job, become very ill, or experience other misfortunes that would make it hard for them to repay the loan. If you lend your $2,000 to just one person, you are putting all your eggs in one basket, as the cheesy but apposite saying goes. Banks can help you spread out your $2,000 so that you are lending a little bit to lots of different borrowers whose risks are uncorrelated—meaning it's unlikely that they will all become unemployed or sick at the same time. So banks perform a valuable role in *diversifying risk*.

Banks are also better placed that any individual saver to assess the risk of lending to specific borrowers. Banks can easily check people's credit history, get an accurate picture of their assets, and figure out what other debts they have. If the potential borrower is a customer of the bank, then the bank knows a lot about their financial history. All this information helps banks decide whom to lend money to and at what interest rate.

Of course, banks don't just lend money belonging to their own customers; they also access what's known as the *wholesale funding market*. That is, banks—which are often big corporations—can issue debt of their own in the bond market. Because of the valuable functions that banks perform in determining whom to lend to, this can be a profitable thing for them to do.

In fact, banks generally have on hand only a fraction of the money that has been deposited with them or lent to them by bondholders. Most of the time that's fine, but in times of crisis lots of depositors might want their money back at the same time. If all banks are holding only, say, ten cents of every dollar on deposit, they won't have enough money on hand to pay everyone who wants to withdraw their funds. When depositors realize this, they may rush to withdraw their money before others get in ahead of them. This leads to the kind of "bank run" that occurred during the Great Depression in many countries.[2]

A lesson from this era was that fear of bank failures can become a self-fulfilling prophecy: an otherwise sound financial institution can become insolvent purely because people believe it is going to become insolvent. The policy response was to establish *deposit insurance*, by which the government guarantees the safety of depositors' money. This is done in the United States through the Federal Deposit Insurance Corporation (FDIC), and other countries have similar schemes. Deposit insurance stops the vicious cycle of panic withdrawals that lead to bank failure and more withdrawals.

But the financial system has become more complicated since the 1930s. Now there can be bank runs on less traditional financial institutions.

Investment banks like JPMorgan Chase and Goldman Sachs don't take money from depositors but lend and borrow through a range of instruments on the wholesale market. Often these loans are short term—as little as twenty-four to forty-eight hours. Again, in normal times that's no problem. The lenders—typically other financial institutions—just roll over their loans. But during a panic, lenders can all want their money back at once. And just as with the regular commercial banks during the Great Depression, the belief that everyone else might want to get their money out can cause otherwise sound institutions to suffer a run.

This is exactly what happened during the financial crisis of 2008, and it's why the US Federal Reserve had to step in to shore up institutions like JPMorgan and Goldman Sachs. Although this emergency intervention was extraordinary, the Fed was already providing liquidity to the banking system. In fact, the Fed's involvement in how banks lend to each other is what determines interest rates—the price of money.

How Central Banks Set Interest Rates

Although I focus here on the US Federal Reserve—partly because it's the most important central bank in the world—this explanation applies broadly to other nations' central banks as well.

Banks are required by the Fed to keep a certain percentage of funds on hand in order to be able to make payments to customers. These funds are known as *reserves*. But sometimes one bank doesn't have quite enough reserves on hand to settle all their payments, and other banks have more than they need. So the banks lend to each other overnight through the *interbank loans market*. The price in this market—determined by supply and demand—is called the *federal funds rate* because it's the price of the funds needed by banks to meet the Fed's reserve requirements.

The federal funds rate is set by the Fed—or more precisely, by its Federal Open Market Committee (FOMC). It's probably the single most important price of anything in the world—much more important than the price of gold, bitcoin, wheat, or Apple stock. The federal funds rate is the benchmark short-term interest rate in the United States. It serves as the basis of the interest rates for car loans and mortgages. Banks charge additional interest depending on their assessment of the risk of the loan they are making.

The Fed can influence the federal funds rate in a number of different ways. First, it can change the amount it pays banks for excess reserves they hold. This sets the minimum interest rate for funds that banks are willing to lend each other in the overnight market, because they could always just leave the funds in their own reserve account and earn the same rate. Second, the Fed itself can borrow funds, which increases demand in the market for overnight loans and pushes up the interest rate. Third, the Fed can lend directly to banks through the *discount window* (so named because in the old days there was a physical window at the Fed through which these loans were made). Banks borrow money from the Fed by posting some kind of asset as collateral. The interest rate for these loans is usually set higher than the federal fund rate, so it acts as a ceiling. By managing both the minimum and maximum interest rates, the Fed can achieve the federal funds rate it wants.

But how can the Fed adjust the minimum interest rate if the federal funds rate is at or near zero? It's not easy for central banks to set negative interest rates—although the European Central Bank (ECB) has experimented with small dips into negative territory—because they mean that people actually lose money by putting it in the bank. Faced with this prospect, people might prefer to keep their money (sometimes literally) under their mattress. This is risky for individuals and also for the banking system, because it puts pressure on the solvency of banks. This makes it harder for banks to lend, which in turn reduces economic activity, pushing the demand for money—and thus interest rates—still lower. This is the kind of deflationary spiral in which Japan got stuck in the 1980s and from which it is still struggling to escape.

This leaves central banks with a problem: they want to cut interest rates to boost economic activity, but they can't move the short-term rate below zero. They are stuck at what is known as the *zero lower bound* on short-term rates. But what about longer-term interest rates? Plenty of loans are made at rates that are fixed for five, ten, fifteen, or even thirty years. Lots of businesses borrow at five- or ten-year rates, and the canonical American mortgage is fixed for thirty years. Can central banks do anything to affect these longer-term rates?

The answer is yes—through setting short-term interest rates. That's because the interest rate on long-term government debt (at least in part) reflects expectations of future short-term rates. So current short-term rates in conjunction with an explicitly announced target for inflation and "forward guidance" about the future path of short-term rates can influence interest rates on longer-term government debt.

But beginning with the financial crisis of 2008, central banks started to take a more direct route to keeping long-term interest rates low. By actually purchasing long-term securities like Treasury bonds—and even privately issued debt such as mortgage-backed securities (MBS)—the Fed could lower the interest rate on them. Fed purchases meant an increase in demand for these securities. Through the basic law of supply and demand, that led to a higher price for the bonds. A higher price for bonds means a lower yield or effective interest rate on them. Other central banks, such as the ECB, took the same approach.

This practice was known interchangeably as *quantitative easing* (QE) and *unconventional monetary policy*. The Federal Reserve would pay for the securities by electronically crediting the bank accounts of the sellers, and those payments would ultimately show up as reserves held by various commercial banks at the Fed.

Some observers were worried that this practice would lead to inflation. They argued that the Fed was, in effect, digitally printing money, thereby expanding the stock of money, or the *money supply*. Ardent believers in a particularly strong form of the monetarist theory pioneered by the Nobel laureate Milton Friedman believed that prices moved in lockstep with the supply of money. They thought doubling bank reserves would double the broader money supply—the money sloshing around in checking and deposit accounts—and lead to a big rise in prices.

This didn't happen. What did happen was that the lower rates on long-term securities affected other lending, giving borrowers more spending power. Yellen, as vice chair of the Fed at that time, commented on this trend in a 2013 speech to the National Association for Business Economics: "There is considerable evidence that these purchases have eased financial conditions, and so have presumably increased interest-sensitive spending. Research suggests that our purchases of mortgage-backed securities pushed down MBS yields and that MBS yields pass through, with a lag, to mortgage rates."[3]

These are the modern tools available to central banks in determining interest rates. How they use them is another matter, and a topic of much controversy.

DIGITAL PAYMENTS

We have already discussed how individual digital payments work, but it is important to understand the system that facilitates those transactions. It might seem completely unremarkable in 2023 that we can walk down a street in New York, London, Sydney, or Paris and securely buy anything from a salad to a refrigerator by looking at the display to unlock our phone and waving it near a small machine in the store. Yet this transaction requires not only advanced communications technology but also an intricate system of handling payments within the banking system.

Of course, paying electronically with credit and debit cards has been possible for many years. The process is fairly straightforward. Merchants who have taken credit card payments that have been authorized send these to a *payment processor*. They pass the details of the transactions to the *card association* (like Visa or Mastercard), which then contacts the bank that issued the card and tells them the amount of the transaction. That issuing bank charges the account of the cardholder and transfers funds to the merchant's bank, which then deposits the funds into the merchant's account. The money has now effectively flowed from your card to the account of the person who sold you a salad.

Big transactions between banks are usually processed via a service provided by the country's central bank. In the United States the service is called Fedwire. It moves funds effectively instantaneously from one deposit-taking institution to another. To settle transactions between banking customers, such as payroll deposits to employees, welfare benefits, tax refunds, mortgage payments, and utility bills, institutions known as *clearinghouses* facilitate electronic payments between banks. In the United States, the regional Federal Reserve banks are the largest clearinghouse operators, and there is also a private clearinghouse known as the Electronic Payments Network.

Until recently, credit and debit card payments left the customer susceptible to various kinds of fraudulent activity at the point of sale. It was easy for an unscrupulous operator to copy card numbers and insecure "security codes"; it was also possible to "skim" account numbers from magnetic strips on credit cards. Services like Apple Pay and Google Pay represent an important increase in security. They replace what Apple's CEO, Tim Cook, described in 2014 as an "antiquated payments process" and an "outdated and vulnerable magnetic interface." [4] With modern payment systems, the merchant has no record of the customer's financial details because a unique security code is used for each transaction.

Despite this progress, there are still significant gaps in the system, and it is precisely these gaps that private digital currencies like libra/diem seek to fill. But first let's look at how mobile money has progressed thus far.

MOBILE MONEY IN THE GLOBAL SOUTH

In some respects it is people in the global South who have been the fastest to adopt and benefit from mobile money. Many people in developing economies don't have bank accounts, and even if they do, they live and work far away from the nearest bank branch. This financial exclusion makes it hard for them to save, invest, and store value. In 2021 there were 1.4 billion adults worldwide without a bank account or access to mobile money. That's a big improvement from 2.1 billion in 2011 and 1.7 billion in 2017 but still a big obstacle to economic activity.[5]

To address the challenges of banking in developing countries, an innovative solution known as *mobile money* has arisen. This system is different from simply accessing a bank account on a mobile phone. Mobile money involves a payment account that resides on the SIM card of a mobile phone and allows the user to perform a variety of financial transactions, including direct person-to-person payments, paying bills, saving, receiving wages, and receiving government benefit payments.

Mobile money emerged in the 2010s in countries like the Philippines, Kenya, and Tanzania. Its spread around the world has been rapid: by 2015 there were 271 mobile money services in ninety-three countries.[6] In 2021, $1 trillion in mobile money transactions was processed for 1.35 billion accounts in ninety-eight countries.[7]

Mobile money is both a massive improvement over having no banking facilities and a long way from the kind of frictionless experience that a cashless society provides. It involves significant transaction fees and relies on often uncompetitive telecommunications markets.

One of the most successful rollouts of mobile money has been in Kenya. By the end of 2014 the uptake of mobile money outside the capital, Nairobi, was a staggering 96 percent. Mobile money in Kenya is known as M-Pesa, with the *M* standing for "mobile" and *pesa* being the Swahili word for "money." M-Pesa began in 2007, offered through the largest Kenyan telecommunications company, Safaricom.[8] Central to its

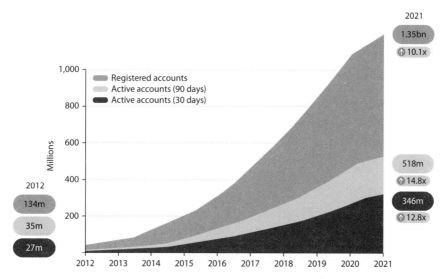

Figure 2. Number of registered and active mobile money accounts worldwide, 2012–2021. *Source:* GSM Association, *State of the Industry Report on Mobile Money*, 10th ed., 2022, www.gsma.com/sotir/wp-content/uploads/2022/03/GSMA_State_of_the_Industry_2022_English.pdf.

success is a network of agents who serve as the functional equivalent of ATMs. Agents buy an initial quantity of e-money from Safaricom and can sell it back or buy more. Since 2009 banks have been allowed to serve as agents, effectively integrating mobile-money agents into the banking system. The economic impact of M-Pesa has been significant and rapid.

One way that M-Pesa improves economic (and social) outcomes is by facilitating risk sharing. In the absence of significant state-provided welfare benefits or insurance schemes, informal risk-sharing networks are important in developing economies. Households have relational contracts (arrangements that are not legally binding but are enforced by reputational and social norms) to transfer money to others who suffer financial shock, such as family illness or job loss. M-Pesa enables people without bank accounts to bypass the significant transaction costs of financial transfers. This means that money in the network flows more efficiently to those in need. Two of the leading scholars of mobile money, William Jack and Tavneet Suri, have shown that households with access to M-Pesa that suffer an adverse shock receive more money and get it from a more diverse set of households in their network. The ease of transferring funds over long distances diversifies and enlarges the risk-sharing network. A large share of M-Pesa transactions are between people (rather than businesses) over long geographic distances.[9]

M-Pesa users are also able to respond better to health shocks, with evidence showing that, relative to nonusers, they increase outlays on medical expenses without sacrificing spending on food and education. Non M-Pesa households, by contrast, tend to decrease spending on food and, according to one careful study, "might pull children out of school to finance healthcare costs."[10]

Perhaps the most striking implication of M-Pesa adoption is that it pulls people out of poverty—leading to a full 2 percentage point decline (nearly two hundred thousand households) in the number of households in poverty in Kenya. And the reduction in poverty was large for female-headed households, in part because access to M-Pesa led to changes in occupation, with 186,000 women moving from the agriculture sector to business and retail.[11]

This all paints a picture of great success, but existing mobile money services have limitations. For one thing, they are largely limited to person-to-person transfers. Mobile money has achieved dramatically lower penetration in other spheres, such as personal-to-business, business-to-business, and government-to-person transfers. In this sense it does not represent a complete—or even nearly complete—payment system.

In order for mobile money to become a full-fledged payment system, people need to have access to all their money all the time, and be able to transfer that in close to real time. Payments need to be widely accepted within the local economy, and transaction fees need to be low. Unfortunately, mobile money falls short on a number of these grounds.

First, the agent network, though a vital part of the current system, is also a bottleneck. M-Pesa agents need to have their own bank accounts. If they have insufficient credits to meet their customers' requests for funds, they have to buy more from Safaricom. They can be credit constrained, making it impossible for them to provide sufficient liquidity. They are typically closer to customers than bank branches but can still be some distance away.

Agents are also privy to their customers' personal information, such as their name, government identification number, and mobile phone number. There are security issues pertaining to individuals or businesses holding that information and to the technology underpinning mobile money.

Finally, the companies that are central to mobile-money systems wield considerable market power, which enables them to charge significant transaction fees. These add friction to the system.

It was these shortcomings of mobile money systems that enabled Facebook to make the seemingly altruistic claim that in introducing libra, a global stable coin, they just wanted to help people in developing economies. Their marketing materials used phrases such as "Moving money around the world should be as easy and cheap as sending a message. No matter where you live, what you do, or how much you earn." They referred to establishing "an open and competitive network" and lamented that "around the world 1.7 billion people are unbanked."[12]

Mobile money has done tremendous economic and social good in developing economies, but there is a long way to go before people in the global South have access to advanced payment systems. And it will be a long, long wait before Swedish-style point-of-sale equipment and an Australian-style payment platform appear across sub-Saharan Africa. But a shortcut to financial liberation exists in the form of a private digital currency. And this is why, even though Facebook failed in establishing a global stable coin, their first attempt won't be the last.

4

CRYPTO

SATOSHI

Not many people noticed an obscure eight-page "white paper" (nine, counting references) by an unknown author, Satoshi Nakamoto, posted on October 28, 2008.[1] Then, as now, the author was a ghost. But what he, she, or they left behind was a breathtakingly clever idea—the basis for a decentralized "crypto" currency. The currency, named bitcoin, replaced a centralized issuing authority (like a bank or government) with a computer network, and it replaced trust with cryptography. Hence the moniker *crypto*.

In retrospect it's easy to see the motivation for a cryptocurrency at that time. The financial crisis was in full swing. The US investment bank Lehman Brothers had collapsed on September 15, sending financial markets into chaos. The next day the Reserve Primary Fund—the original money-market fund, which had been around since 1970—"broke the buck": investors were told they would only receive ninety-seven cents on the dollar for their holdings. This scenario was thought to be impossible. Yet here we were. Banks with names that defined Wall Street—Goldman Sachs and JP Morgan—looked set to fail, at one point losing more than a third of their value in one day's trading.

The US Treasury and Federal Reserve managed to engineer a bailout costing more than $1 trillion that saved the world financial system from collapse, but ordinary Americans were hammered. Retirement savings were savaged, and around six million Americans lost their homes to foreclosure, as did many people involved in property bubbles in Spain, Ireland, and other countries.

But those losses—devastating though they were—weren't the most serious consequences of the financial crisis. Public confidence in the financial system was shattered and has not recovered. How could anyone have confidence in the big banks who had not just allowed the market for mortgage-backed securities to grow out of control but turbocharged it with financial incentives? How could anyone trust the people who invented financial instruments like collateralized debt obligations and credit default swaps that blew up the financial system and the real economy with it? And how could we trust the regulators and government authorities who hadn't seen the trouble coming, an attitude captured best by Fed chair Ben Bernanke's remark in mid-May 2007: "We believe the effect of the troubles in the subprime sector on the broader housing market will be limited, and we do not expect significant spillovers from the subprime market to the rest of the economy or to the financial system."[2]

To be fair, Bernanke did a remarkable job in steering the American and global economy out of the crisis. And he wasn't responsible for either the bad behavior of the private sector or the fact that bailing out the banks at taxpayer expense was the only way to resolve the crisis. But the failures of foresight by regulators contributed to public anger.

It was in this wreckage of public confidence in centralized financial institutions that the idea of a cryptocurrency took root. And although it wasn't hard to see why a decentralized currency would be appealing, it was hard to anticipate the genius of Nakamoto's idea.

There's a saying in academic writing: "Now that you've written your conclusion, you know how to write your introduction."[3] Nakamoto may not have been privy to this piece of wisdom, but the conclusion to the white paper is a succinct explanation of how a cryptocurrency might operate.

> We have proposed a system for electronic transactions without relying on trust. We started with the usual framework of coins made from digital signatures, which provides strong control of ownership, but is incomplete without a way to prevent double-spending. To solve this, we proposed a peer-to-peer network using proof-of-work to record a public history of transactions that quickly becomes computationally impractical for an attacker to change if honest nodes control a majority of CPU power. The network is robust in its unstructured simplicity. Nodes work all at once with little coordination. . . . They vote with their CPU power, expressing their acceptance of valid blocks by working on extending them and rejecting invalid blocks by refusing to work on them. Any needed rules and incentives can be enforced with this consensus mechanism.[4]

There are four elements to this cryptocurrency. First, there are coins. These, as Nakamoto says, are familiar. Coins can just be objects with digital signatures. But many digital objects can be easily duplicated. I could send you a digital coin in exchange for something of value and then go and send the same coin to somebody else. Preventing double spending is the purpose of the second element—the public record of transactions. The *ledger* is a record of all transactions using the digital currency. All the nodes on the network are privy to this ledger, because without a trusted central authority, the ledger has to be public, and all the nodes need to agree on a unique history of transactions.

This is where element 3 comes in—proof of work. Nodes compete to complete a cryptographic problem, and the winner of this competition is asked, though not required, to append a block to the longest chain of blocks. To provide an incentive for nodes to do this, there is a prize for winning this race and validating a block. There are two parts to this prize: a "block reward" and a "transaction fee."[5]

Solving this cryptographic problem requires significant computing power. It is this computational intensity that provides security. To change a past transaction (and make double spending possible), a node would have to deploy enough computing power to modify that transaction as well as all subsequent transactions. Nakamoto proved mathematically that doing so would require a majority of the computing power available on the entire network.[6]

The way that blocks are appended to a chain is the fourth and final element of Nakamoto's cryptocurrency—and it's known as the *longest chain rule*, although it's a convention rather than a rule. As long as there is indeed a longest chain, this acts as a kind of focal point—why not just append your block to the longest chain? The fact that this requires coordination is not completely innocuous and raises the question of what happens if nodes fail to coordinate. This is the issue of *forking* of a blockchain, but we don't need to worry about that here.[7]

The use of computing power to solve cryptographic puzzles has become known as "mining bitcoin." Nakamoto made the analogy to mining gold in his whitepaper, saying: "The steady addition of a constant of amount of new coins is analogous to gold miners expending resources to add gold to circulation. In our case, it is CPU time and electricity that is expended."[8] Bitcoin became a reality on January 3, 2009, when its "genesis block" (the very first block in the bitcoin blockchain), or "block 0," was mined.

The advantage of bitcoin, as Nakamoto pointed out, lies in the decentralized way it establishes trust. When centralized institutions are involved in transactions, these transactions are always open to being disputed and possibly reversed. As Nakamoto observed: "Commerce on the Internet has come to rely almost exclusively on financial institutions serving as trusted third parties to process electronic payments. While the system works well enough for most transactions, it still suffers from the inherent weaknesses of the trust based model. Completely non-reversible transactions are not really possible, since financial institutions cannot avoid mediating disputes."[9] Centralized institutions try to mitigate the likelihood and cost of fraud by collecting information about the parties to a transaction. Bitcoin obviates the need for doing so, and therein lies its appeal to those with a radical distrust of centralized authority such as government or large financial institutions, and a strong desire for privacy.

Although Nakamoto solved an engineering problem, they did it by creating an economic system—a whole, completely new, internally consistent economic system. It's worth pausing to note just how improbable this achievement was. The centralized authorities about whose systems Nakamoto was expressing a breezy contempt were national governments and some of the largest and most influential corporations in the world.

And Nakamoto's engineering solution was rooted in a paradox. If a single central actor having information was a problem—if one entity being untrustworthy was a problem—then how could it be that the solution to that problem was to give everyone the information? The answer is cryptography. The key idea that allows decentralization to work is that blockchains divide changes to the (public) ledger into bite-sized "blocks." This way, changes to the ledger happen at an orderly pace, and blocks are strung or "chained" via cryptographic "hashing."[10] It is this ingredient—the cryptographic hashing—that is key to providing security, since manipulating one block effectively requires manipulating other blocks. And changing any block requires the expenditure of real resources. Under Nakamoto's proof-of-work protocol, these resources are energy. And he matched those costs with just the right

set of benefits—through block rewards and transaction fees—to provide the right incentives for people to validate transactions.

That kind of inventiveness doesn't happen very often. And bitcoin
had a philosophy that was matched to the moment. It was decentralized and hence democratic.

Yet the proposal had two serious flaws. First, the key insight underpinning the idea of the blockchain—that validating blocks had to be
costly—was far from innocuous. Bitcoin mining uses vast amounts of
electricity. In 2022 the energy used to make bitcoin secure was roughly
as much as the entire population of Sweden used in a year. Hashes were
being computed at the rate of about 200 quintillion per second. The
hash rate naturally increases when the price of bitcoin rises, because
when the price of bitcoin, is higher so is the reward, and people are
willing to incur a higher cost—and use more electricity—to chase that
larger reward.

This puts bitcoin on a collision course with itself. The more successful it is—at least if success is measured by the price of bitcoin—then the
more resources it requires to make it secure. This is a problem to which
we will return.

The second flaw was an engineering issue to do with the programming language Nakamoto used. In solving that problem, a Russian-
Canadian prodigy expanded the philosophical reach of blockchain far
beyond "just" money and became an avatar for the crypto movement.

VITALIK

Vitalik Buterin was fourteen years old when the bitcoin whitepaper was
posted, and it was another three years before his computer-scientist
father introduced him to bitcoin. Yet it was Buterin who—in the absence
of a known bitcoin founder—became the face of the crypto movement.

In a 2016 interview, Buterin explained his worldview as a young adult—
one consonant with Nakamoto's distrust of centralized authority: "I saw

everything to do with either government regulation or corporate control as just being plain evil. And I assumed that people in those institutions were kind of like Mr. Burns, sitting behind their desks saying, 'Excellent. How can I screw a thousand people over this time?'"[11]

Buterin took a six-month global tour to learn what people were trying to do with Bitcoin. He then wrote his own white paper. He decided that building applications on top of the bitcoin network was unworkable, because the programming language that Nakamoto had used for the bitcoin protocol was designed exclusively for cryptocurrency: it was deliberately limited in the nature and complexity of the transactions it could handle.

There was a single-minded elegance to this design choice, but it revealed a lack of insight about economics. Money—even digital money—is useful as a store and value and a means of exchange. But what makes money *really* useful is that it helps form the basis of contracts between two parties. Nondigital money has shaped the institutions that have facilitated contracting over centuries, such as contract law, the design of securities such as debt and equity, and governance arrangements like the limited liability corporation.

Without accounting for these institutions, Bitcoin could not function as the basis of nonmonetary transactions. And since the animating premise of bitcoin was that traditional, centralized institutions were not to be trusted, if bitcoin was to be internally consistent, it would need to develop its own set of contracting institutions to parallel those of the nondigital world.

Satoshi Nakamoto had designed bitcoin in a way that essentially prevented the development of these digital institutions. They had come up with an idea so ingenious and timely that a growing community of crypto believers was hooked. And then they had vanished.

Buterin had a solution. In his 2013 white paper he outlined a version of bitcoin based on what computer scientists call a "universal" or "Turing-complete" programming language—that is, a programming language that can compute anything that any other computational method can compute.[12] Most programming languages, including Java, Python, and C++, are universal. He called his invention Ethereum.

Ethereum combined all the features of a programming language with the properties of a cryptocurrency that Nakamoto had outlined. Buterin named his cryptocurrency ether (ETH).

By allowing a whole set of decentralized institutions to exist in a system in which exchanges could occur, Buterin ushered in a philosophical revolution. His white paper began by posing the question of "how the blockchain concept can be used for more than just money." His examples included "using on-blockchain digital assets to represent custom currencies and financial instruments ('colored coins'), the ownership of an underlying physical device ('smart property'), non-fungible assets such as domain names ('Namecoin') as well as more advanced applications such as decentralized exchange, financial derivatives, peer-to-peer gambling and on-blockchain identity and reputation systems."[13]

Then he mentioned smart contracts, or "systems which automatically move digital assets according to arbitrary pre-specified rules" and what he saw as the "logical extension" of smart contracts: "decentralized autonomous organizations (DAOs)."[14] Buterin understood what economists have emphasized for some time—that organizations are fundamentally contracts of one form or another.[15] As he put it, DAOs are "long-term smart contracts that contain the assets and encode the bylaws of an entire organization." And he clarified that combining a blockchain with a programming language was the key to creating a vast range of contracts, and hence organizations. The end of Buterin's introduction read: "What Ethereum intends to provide is a blockchain with a built-in fully fledged Turing-complete programming language that can be used to create 'contracts' that can be used to encode arbitrary state transition functions, allowing users to create any of the systems described above, as well as many others that we have not yet imagined, simply by writing up the logic in a few lines of code."[16]

One of the advantages of smart contracts is that they can be protected against renegotiation. A smart contract has two interesting properties that a regular, paper-based contract (I will resist the temptation to call it a "dumb" contract) does not have. First, it is self-executing. It is literally a bunch of computer code that takes certain inputs, follows a set of commands, and produces certain outputs, such as a transfer of funds between contracting parties. Second, smart contracts on a blockchain permit irreversible transfers to anonymous accounts. Even if you know the person you are contracting with, as far as any third party is concerned, that individual is just an account code. A court of law can issue a person a subpoena to appear in a court proceeding, but it cannot subpoena an account code.

Smart contracts offer a way for contracting parties to commit to a certain outcome. In many situations, if contracting parties can't write a contract that provides for all possible future contingencies, then they might not be able to reach an agreement to transact. This is known as the "hold-up problem," and it is central to understanding why some economic activity takes place in firms and other activity takes place in markets. It also helps explain why government sometimes owns certain key strategic assets.[17] The hold-up problem flows from the combination of "incomplete contracts" and the inability of contracting parties to commit *not* to renegotiate their contract. And this means that economic efficiency is sacrificed, at least to some degree. Smart contracts offer a potential solution by allowing parties to structure their strategic interaction using *renegotiation-design mechanisms*.[18]

A decentralized set of organizations based on blockchain technology forms the basis of a conception of the internet known as Web 3.0 or Web3. It contrasts with the original World Wide Web (or Web 1.0), lasting from approximately 1991 to 2004, which consisted of largely static webpages, and with Web 2.0, which is the current (as of 2023) incarnation, involving social and commercial interactions on centralized platforms such as Facebook, Amazon, Uber, and Twitter.

It's fair to say Web3 is a vision of the future rather than of the present. This brings us to the question of how useful cryptocurrencies like bitcoin and ether are right now—and hence what their intrinsic value is.

HOW USEFUL IS CRYPTO?

A lot of smart people—from the legendary investor Warren Buffett to US Treasury Secretary Janet Yellen, and economics Nobel laureates like Paul Krugman, Oliver Hart, and Eric Maskin—have expressed extreme skepticism about the value of cryptocurrencies, at least as they are constituted today.

Buffett told his Berkshire Hathaway investors at their 2022 annual meeting that "If you . . . owned all of the bitcoin in the world and you offered it to me for $25, I wouldn't take it. . . . Because what would I do with it? I'll have to sell it back to you one way or another. It isn't going to do anything."[19] Yellen remarked in 2021: "I don't think that bitcoin . . . is widely used as a transaction mechanism. . . . To the extent it is used I fear it's often for illicit finance. It's an extremely inefficient way of conducting transactions, and the amount of energy that's consumed in processing those transactions is staggering."[20]

In a 2021 *New York Times* column, Paul Krugman—in typically acerbic fashion—observed that "cryptocurrencies play almost no role in normal economic activity. Almost the only time we hear about them being used as a means of payment—as opposed to speculative trading—is in association with illegal activity."[21] Earlier, in 2018, he predicted that "once the dream of a blockchained future dies, the disappointment will probably collapse the whole thing."[22] Oliver Hart put it this way: "I don't understand Bitcoin. Economic theory tells us it should be worthless, but it is not. I still think it's a bubble which will burst."[23] Eric Maskin was even blunter, opining that "Bitcoin has a fundamental value of $0."[24]

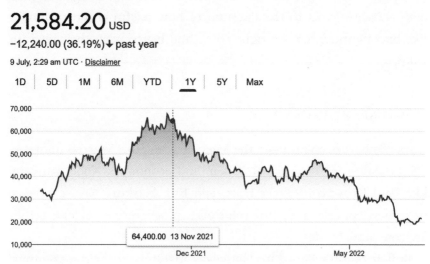

Figure 3. Bitcoin price, 9 July 2021–9 July 2022. *Source:* Google Finance, www.google.com/finance/ quote/BTC-USD.

There are certainly problems with bitcoin (and other cryptocurrencies). One is its volatility. Figure 3 shows the wild swings in its value against the dollar from mid-2021 to mid-2022. This makes bitcoin a bad store of value. Bitcoin and other cryptocurrencies are also very difficult, and costly, to use for everyday transactions (except maybe for buying frozen yoghurt in Keene, New Hampshire). Although a few prominent companies, like Tesla and Microsoft, have announced plans to accept bitcoin, those have been largely publicity-driven exercises. (Tesla reversed the decision just two months after announcing it.) A *New York Times* journalist tried to buy a pack of N95 face masks from Amazon with bitcoin, using an application called Purse. The sticker price of the masks was $42.99, but the equivalent price in bitcoin was $47.47.[25] That's a 10.4 percent markup. So even when it's possible to make ordinary purchases with bitcoin, it's an expensive way to shop.

There are a number of rejoinders to these criticisms of cryptocurrencies. If you want to trade illicit goods like drugs or arms, then it may be worth paying the additional transaction costs to avoid detection by law enforcement authorities. The same goes for using cryptocurrency for tax evasion. But these activities make a stronger case for regulating or banning cryptocurrencies than for using them.

Buterin's vision of a set of decentralized organizations built on smart contracts provides an alternative and potentially highly socially productive rationale for cryptocurrencies. In fact, some people who occupy the middle ground between crypto–true believer and intense crypto-skeptics (like the aforementioned economists) base their view of the value of cryptocurrencies on potential uses in smart-contracting applications.

A more basic rationale for crypto goes back to its roots: crypto doesn't require trust in *anyone*. After the Russian invasion of Ukraine, Buterin noted that "blockchain is at its core a security technology—a technology that is fundamentally all about protecting people and helping them survive in such an unfriendly world."[26] Alluding to *The Lord of the Rings*, he called it "'a light to you in dark places, when all other lights go out.' . . . It is not a low-cost light, or a fluorescent hippie energy-efficient light, or a high-performance light. It is a light that sacrifices on *all* of those dimensions to optimize for one thing and one thing only: *to be a light that does when [sic] it needs to do when you're facing the toughest challenge of your life and there is a friggin twenty foot spider staring at you in the face.*"[27]

Ultimately, the usefulness of cryptocurrency, as with any currency, depends on how widely it is accepted. Right now US dollars are the dominant medium of exchange in the United States, whether the transactions are in cash or cashless. And this is a self-reinforcing equilibrium, similar to the convention whereby US drivers keep to the right-hand side of the road. Even if we don't care about traffic laws, if everyone else is driving on the right-hand side, it is far safer to do the same. And there are lots of laws and institutional features (like the placement of the steering wheel in a car) that support this equilibrium. But other countries, like Australia, drive on the left-hand-side.

Overnight in September 1967, however, Sweden switched from everyone driving on the left-hand side of the road to driving on the right. Could the same thing happen for the primary medium of exchange in a country like the United States? The answer is yes. And it could happen in one of two ways: a country could establish an official digital currency through its central bank, or a private company could establish its own currency. Could a private digital currency achieve widespread acceptance or even displace a currency like the US dollar? Again, the answer is yes. And the likelihood that it could happen is greater than most people think.

PRIVATE DIGITAL CURRENCIES AND STABLE COINS

The central fact about any medium of exchange is that it involves network externalities: its value to an individual consumer depends, in part, on how many other consumers participate in the market. If lots of people use the US dollar as a medium of exchange, then it's attractive for me to do so. Lots of sellers accept US dollars precisely because many people use them.

This virtuous circle is a feature of many digital markets, and it leads to "winner-take-most" outcomes where there is typically one dominant player with extremely high market share. The clearest examples of this are platforms such as Uber, Facebook, and Amazon. Network externalities are also present in services where machine learning leads to product innovation, such as internet search (Google) or music (Apple Music or Spotify). And they are also present in hardware underpinned by ecosystem-specific apps such as Apple's and Google's app stores.

There is nothing very special about the US dollar. It has a lot of legal and institutional backing. It has a long and venerable history. But the fact that we all use it owes a lot to convention and circumstance. Or, in the language of economists, everyone using the US dollar is just one equilibrium in a coordination game where there are multiple possible equilibria.

To underscore this point, let's think about another example—ridesharing, where Uber has a roughly 70 percent market share and Lyft has a 30 percent share.[28] Now suppose that Uber raised its price for all trips by 15 percent, perhaps in an effort to capitalize on its high market share. One of two things might happen. It might be that Uber riders really value the large size of the Uber network, which means that they have to wait for a shorter time to get a ride. If that's worth enough to them, then most Uber riders might just pay the higher fares and stick with Uber rather than switch to Lyft. They wouldn't be happy about it, but it would be in their own best interest to stay with Uber.

Alternatively, some current Uber riders might decide that they'd prefer to wait a minute or two longer for a Lyft than pay the higher price for an Uber. The number of "likely defectors" could be relatively small, but it could lead other riders to realize that with other people switching to Lyft, they are going to face slightly longer wait times for Uber rides. They may conclude that the 15 percent premium isn't worth it for this slightly less good service, and they'll switch to Lyft. This shift might trigger a type of unraveling, making another group of Uber riders realize that they're paying 15 percent more for a service that now has even longer wait times. By the force of economic logic, these initial ripples of consumers willing to switch from Uber to Lyft may lead to a wave of riders making the move. All of a sudden, the attempt by Uber to exploit its high market share by raising prices could lead to a shift in equilibrium where it becomes the player with 30 percent market share and Lyft holds 70 percent of the market.

This phenomenon can be formalized and made mathematically precise, as Robert Akerlof, Luis Rayo, and I have shown.[29] What matters is the relative price and relative quality of the products offered by the two competing companies. So let's apply this logic to the market for money.

In the market for transactions in the United States—paying for goods and services—the US dollar currently has an overwhelmingly dominant share relative to bitcoin. In fact, the use of cryptocurrencies for transactions involving goods and services is so small it's hard to measure. There's a large market for buying and selling the cryptocurrencies themselves—Bitcoin processed $3 trillion worth of transactions in 2021, more than double what American Express did.[30] But only a small fraction of those transactions involved buying "stuff." BitPay—one of the largest crypto payments processors—processed about $1 billion worth of transactions in 2021.[31] But BitPay processes transactions for companies like AT&T and Microsoft, and bitcoin accounts for only about two-thirds of those transactions. By comparison, more than $72.6 *trillion* worth of transactions were processed by the ACH network for digital payments, run by the Federal Reserve banks and the private-sector operator EPN.[32]

How could the situation change so that the US dollar was no longer the dominant medium for exchange? It might look a lot like what Facebook proposed with its libra stable coin (which morphed into diem). Although diem suffered a fatal setback when Treasury Secretary Janet Yellen refused to support it, that doesn't mean that a related model couldn't succeed. Indeed, Yellen's refusal to support diem suggests that she saw a private digital currency as a potentially serious competitor to the US dollar, and hence to the US Treasury.

The idea of private digital currencies goes back to at least 1994, when Edward de Bono wrote of the "IBM dollar."[33] In de Bono's vision, "large manufacturing corporations" should create their own currencies, which could be used to buy their products. He saw this scheme chiefly as a way for companies to smooth out the volatility of sales and make their business more predictable.

The Libra Stable Coin Model

The original white paper that outlined libra appeared in mid 2019.[34] It starts with a crisp and stark statement of at least one important problem: there are 1.7 billion people in the world who have no access to banking services, despite the fact that 1 billion of those people have a mobile phone and 500 million of them have internet access. Those who can least afford it often pay very high transaction fees for access to money, including wire, overdraft, and ATM withdrawal fees. The issue extends to advanced economies, where people often pay annualized interest rates as high as 400 percent on payday loans. The solution proposed in the white paper is "Libra"—a "simple global currency and financial infrastructure" to "deliver on the promise of 'the internet of money.'" The currency would be stored in "Calibra" digital wallets operated by a regulated subsidiary entity.

The proposal contained three core elements:

1. A global currency (libra) built on a specific kind of blockchain technology.
2. Backing by a diversified reserve of assets intended to make the currency stable.
3. Governance by an "independent" entity—the Libra Association.[35]

The list of founding members was impressive. It included payments companies like Mastercard, Visa, PayPal, and Stripe; technology companies like eBay, Facebook, Spotify, and Uber; telcos like Vodafone; blockchain players like Anchorage, Coinbase, and Xapo; venture capital funds like Andreesen Horowitz, Breakthrough Initiative, and Union Square Ventures; and nonprofit organizations like the Creative Destruction Lab.

The Libra Blockchain

The blockchain on which libra was to be based had a number of features designed to make it highly secure and able to serve billions of users. The vision included not just a currency but a platform akin to Buterin's vision for Ethereum, capable of providing financial and other services. A specific programming language, Move, was designed with the core goal of making smart contracts secure. To prevent digital assets of any kind from being "cloned," they were required to have some of the properties of physical assets. Specifically, a resource would have a single owner, it could be spent only once, and the creation of new resources would be restricted. Move would be designed to ensure that smart contracts couldn't smuggle in nefarious features: it required "that transactions satisfy certain properties, such as payment transactions only changing the account balances of the payer and receiver."[36]

The consensus protocol that it planned to use was *proof of stake* (POS) rather than *proof of work* (POW). In principle, this approach would not require the extremely high energy usage of POW, and it would make the network more resistant to malicious attacks. These were two distinct features. POS essentially relies on voting to validate the blocks. The security aspect involves what is known as *Byzantine fault tolerance* (BFT). As I put it in a paper with Joshua Gans, this contrasts with the longest-chain-rule approach (used by bitcoin) in the following way: "A proposed block is considered confirmed if at least two thirds of validators have sent a message 'agreeing' to the proposed block. . . . Future proposed blocks must then be chained to the last confirmed block."[37]

Libra also had features, disturbing to regulators, that would ensure privacy. It would allow users to be anonymous and possess multiple internet addresses. The white paper noted that the Libra Association would "continue to evaluate new techniques that enhance privacy in the blockchain while considering concerns of practicality, scalability, and regulatory impact."[38] Such anonymity permits all kinds of troubling things to happen. There was one other gremlin in the details of the libra blockchain: it was, at least in the first instance, "permissioned." Blockchains can be either *permissionless* (meaning anyone can join), or *permissioned* (meaning users must be granted access). Permissioning initially made sense. After all, what if a group calling itself Friends of Putin wanted to join and start validating transactions—or obstructing them? But how and why would the libra blockchain transition from being permissioned to permissionless? Why would the original members give up power?

The Libra Reserve

The libra founders acknowledged that a major problem with existing cryptocurrencies was their volatility. Libra's stated goals were "stability, low inflation, wide global acceptance, and fungibility."[39]

A key plank in achieving these goals was the Libra Reserve. The funds generated from selling libra would be invested in a reserve fund of assets "such as bank deposits and short-term government securities in currencies from stable and reputable central banks." This, the founders thought, would help give holders of libra "a high degree of assurance they can convert their digital currency into local fiat currency based on an exchange rate, just like exchanging one currency for another when traveling."[40]

Indeed, the founders claimed that "the assets behind Libra are the major difference between it and many existing cryptocurrencies that lack such intrinsic value and hence have prices that fluctuate significantly based on expectations."[41] Yet during an acute financial crisis, this kind of asset backing does not prevent a modern-day bank run. In 2008 the Reserve Primary Fund fell prey to exactly this kind of panic when the supposedly impossible happened and it "broke the buck." In the crypto crash of 2022, stable coins that were supposedly fully backed fell below their theoretical value. The largest of these—and hence the most surprising failure—was tether, with a market capitalization of $82 billion. Tether, like other stable coins, was essentially acting as a money-market fund but wasn't regulated as one. There were widespread concerns that the failure of tether could crater the entire crypto market.[42]

Janet Yellen again saw the issue clearly, saying that stable coins involve "the same kind of risks that we have known for centuries in connection with bank runs."[43] In testimony to the House Financial Services Committee, Yellen pointed to the need for stronger regulation, noting that "digital assets may pose risks to the financial system, and increased and coordinated regulatory attention is necessary. On March 9, 2022, President Biden signed an Executive Order calling for comprehensive approach to digital asset policy. The [Financial Stability Oversight] Council is drafting a report that will identify financial stability risks and regulatory gaps. I look forward to working with you on the issues and opportunities posed by digital assets. We are also eager to work with you to ensure that payment stable coins and their arrangements are subject to a federal prudential framework on a consistent and comprehensive basis."[44] As if to underline this point, the so-called algorithmic stable coin terraUSD, which had a $16 billion market capitalization and was designed to maintain a 1: 1 value with the US dollar, also broke the buck in early May 2022.[45]

The Libra Association

Ironically (some might say incongruously), even though Libra would be built on a decentralized ledger, it needed a governing authority to manage the evolution of the blockchain technology and the reserve. This authority was to be a not-for-profit group composed of founding members, headquartered in Geneva, Switzerland. As the white paper stated: "Switzerland has a history of global neutrality and openness to blockchain technology, and the association strives to be a neutral, international institution, hence the choice to be registered there."[46] This was surely more to do with optics than with the power of law.

According to the proposal, a two-thirds majority of the founding members would be required to approve major policy or technical decisions, and the governing authority would be the only entity able to mint or destroy libra. The white paper also anticipated (at least for a time) "additional roles that need to be performed on behalf of the association: the recruitment of Founding Members to serve as validator nodes; the design and implementation of incentive programs to propel the adoption of Libra, including the distribution of such incentives to Founding Members; and the establishment of the association's social impact grant-making program."[47]

How Much Power Would Libra Have Had?

Taken at face value (and accepting some of the language used in the white paper), libra would have been a "public good." And the white paper was full of feel-good statements such as "People have an inherent right to control the fruit of their legal labor," "We believe that global, open, instant, and low-cost movement of money will create immense economic opportunity and more commerce across the world," and "We all have a responsibility to help advance financial inclusion, support ethical actors, and continuously uphold the integrity of the ecosystem." But these sententious statements obscured the enormous underlying power that the Libra Association, and therefore Facebook, would have had. Facebook was central to the idea of libra. According to the white paper, "While final decision-making authority rests with the association, Facebook is expected to maintain a leadership role through 2019."[48]

Consider what would have happened if Facebook's CEO, Mark Zuckerberg, had made a public statement along the following lines: "Despite our best intentions, enormous effort, and great goodwill, the governance of libra has become unworkable. We created libra to provide financial inclusion to the world's most disadvantaged people. But libra no longer serves that noble goal. In good conscience I cannot allow Facebook to continue to support it. Effective immediately we will be returning all funds contained in Calibra wallets to their rightful owners—information Calibra and only Calibra has. As soon as this process is complete, we will be withdrawing from the Libra Association, and we expect other founding members of goodwill to do likewise."

That would have been the end of libra. And it would have been a threat that only Facebook—given its unique status as core founder and its enormous customer base—could make. So, faced with the prospect of Facebook delivering that message, would votes on the Libra Association be arm's length? Or would other members basically go along with what Facebook wanted? Any game theorist or political realist knows the answer to that question and the implicit power Facebook would have had over libra.

Of course, Facebook might never have needed to make that threat, much less deliver on it. Between them, the members of the Libra Association would have had the power to extract extraordinary value and concessions from governments around the world. They could decide to add or remove a country's currency from the Libra Reserve, with significant implications for interest rates, capital flight, and financial stability in that country. Even a modest reweighting—something that would necessarily happen from time to time—would serve as a powerful warning. Countries do preferential corporate-tax deals all the time. It would have been easy for Libra Association members to extract concessional corporate-tax rates in exchange for cooperation regarding the Libra Reserve. What's more, this could all have been done with plausible deniability.

Through the Calibra wallet, the Libra Association would implicitly have had the ability to permit or block the use of funds for certain types of transactions, such as those involving contraband or illicit activities. This capability could, of course, be used for good—reducing human trafficking or drug dealing—or it could be used as means to exert power in specific countries. Either way, the Libra Association (or Facebook) would have power over meaningful democratic policy choices.

None of this should be terribly surprising. Money is power, and just because an entity with control over much of the world's money expresses good intentions—or at least creates a system with positive byproducts, like financial inclusiveness—doesn't mean it won't have enormous political leverage. And the hard truth is that, despite having the backing of the Fed chair, Jay Powell, and a mountain of powerful corporations, as well as a compelling pitch about financial inclusion, the libra/diem proposal went down because of Facebook's earlier misuse of its power, in particular the stink associated with its role in the 2016 US presidential election.

BEZOS BUCKS, GOOGLE GOLD, OR APPLES?

The libra/diem proposal had a lot of appealing features along with socially problematic aspects. How might another a private digital currency might succeed where libra did not?

To take advantage of network externalities, it is important to be able to attract a large block of customers quickly. This is sometimes referred to as "getting the flywheel going"—that is, operating on a large enough scale that the positive benefits to consumers from network externalities kick in quickly. Facebook's user base would perhaps have provided such a block of customers, but there is some psychological distance between social media and money. Other potential backers of a private digital currency arguably have considerably greater proximity in product space than Facebook did. An important early paper by Joshua Gans and Hanna Halaburda on private digital currencies pointed out that "any currency can be viewed as a platform"—and it is the attractiveness of the platform on which its adoption depends.[49]

Consider Amazon, with 197 million visitors to its site every month. It has annualized sales revenue of about $400 billion a year. A staggering 95 million Americans have an Amazon Prime membership—a service that offers discounted or free shipping in exchange for a $139 annual fee, making Amazon their effective default shopping option for a vast range of merchandise.[50] This large, sticky, customer base makes it plausible that Amazon could launch its own digital currency. Borrowing a few pages from the libra playbook, it might look like this.

The currency would have four pillars. The first involves the Amazon platform. Amazon would announce that from now on, while users could continue to pay by credit card for purchases, they could also use a digital currency called *amazons* (I like *Bezos bucks* or *BBs*, but that might be a bridge too far, even for Jeff Bezos). Customers could convert US dollars into Amazons—and at least for the time being they could convert them back, on demand, at a 1:1 exchange rate, perhaps for a small fee. Using amazons for purchases would give users a discount off the regular purchase price, maybe 2 percent. That would give folks an incentive to use amazons. In fact, Amazon already offers a virtual currency called Amazon coins that can be used on the Amazon Appstore to buy certain apps and games and make in-app purchases. So perhaps amazons would look like a natural extension of that.

As a platform that matches buyers and sellers, Amazon has considerable market power and leverage. In principle, Amazon could mandate that sellers had to accept amazons instead of dollars for sales in the Amazon marketplace. Such an arrangement would be unlikely to work in the short term. Amazons would be no use to retailers who need to pay their suppliers in dollars—at least not at the start. But if amazons were in sufficiently widespread use, this would be no problem. The challenge for Amazon would be to drive adoption of their currency without penalizing sellers on their platform, which would impede its core business. The smart approach would be to pay sellers some portion of their sale price in amazons—maybe 10 percent initially—and the rest in dollars. Each seller would have a digital wallet into which amazons would be paid. The amazons could be converted frictionlessly into dollars.

This approach would create a subtle but useful default for Amazon. Although it would not be hard for sellers to convert their amazons to dollars, the presence of amazons in their digital wallet, ready to be spent elsewhere on the Amazon platform, would offer an incentive to use them. Paying interest on funds saved in the wallet would motivate sellers to park their money in an Amazon digital wallet rather than transferring it to their bank and earning close to zero interest there. The introduction of these features would provide a natural way for Amazon to offer other financial services for small businesses (subject to some of the regulatory issues discussed below).

Pillar 2 involves Amazon Web Services (AWS). AWS is the world's largest cloud-computing company. It started out as a means of running Amazon's own platform and has since grown into a company that offers similar services to other companies and even university researchers. Netflix is AWS's largest customer. Not far behind, in terms of monthly spending, are Twitch and Linkedin. Other major companies that run a significant part of their business on AWS include Facebook/Meta (for third-party collaborations with existing AWS users), Turner Broadcasting, BBC, ESPN, and Baidu.

Requiring these very significant companies who are AWS customers to hold amazons—without any sweetener—would be similar to saying that those companies had to pay in advance for AWS services rather than being billed on commercial terms. It would be like a straight transfer of working capital between AWS and its customers—for the benefit of AWS. Such an approach, incurring extra costs to the customers, would be unlikely to succeed. But Amazon/AWS could offer a form of partnership with some or all of these big companies, similar in some ways to the idea of the Libra Association. The libra white paper envisioned bringing on board major payments companies like Visa, Mastercard, PayPal, and Stripe. This would increase the likelihood of a private digital currency taking hold.

But when Visa and other payments companies dropped out of the Libra Association in October 2019, they had two key concerns.[51] The first was whether the Libra Association would fully comply with regulatory requirements. During a House Financial Services Committee hearing into the plans for libra, the head of the project at Facebook, David Marcus, was essentially asked by Rep. Maxine Waters (D-CA) whether the company would wait for Congress to consider appropriate regulation. Marcus replied, "I committed to waiting for us to have all the appropriate regulatory approvals and have addressed all concerns before moving forward." Waters said, "That's not a commitment." Marcus seemed to be suggesting that Facebook would comply with existing regulations, whereas lawmakers on the committee had made clear throughout the hearing that an innovation of this magnitude could require significant new regulations.[52]

While much of the questioning in this October 2019 hearing focused on libra, it occurred against the backdrop of serious concerns among some members about Facebook's reputation and past behavior, including its involvement in the Cambridge Analytica scandal. Cambridge Analytica was a British company which, during the 2010s, collected a trove of personal data from Facebook users without their consent and used them for political advertising purposes.

These concerns were most crisply verbalized by Rep. Alexandria Ocasio-Cortez (D-NY), nicknamed AOC, who said to Zuckerberg: "I think you of all people can appreciate using a person's past behavior in order to determine, predict, or make decisions about future behavior. In order for us to make decisions about Libra I think we need to kind of dig into your past behavior, Facebook's past behavior, with respect to our democracy. Ah, Mr. Zuckerberg, what year and month did you personally first become aware of Cambridge Analytica?"[53]

By the time of this exchange Visa had already withdrawn from the Libra Association, issuing the following statement: "[Visa] will continue to evaluate and our ultimate decision will be determined by a number of factors, including the Association's ability to fully satisfy all requisite regulatory expectations. Visa's continued interest in Libra stems from our belief that well-regulated blockchain-based networks could extend the value of secure digital payments to a greater number of people and places, particularly in emerging and developing markets."[54]

This exchange points to the vital importance of reputation in attracting corporate users of a private digital currency. A sticky customer base may be sufficient to attract consumers, but major companies like Visa, Netflix, or ESPN need to be confident that participation will enhance, not diminish, their reputation. Despite its remarkable successes, Facebook simply had too much baggage, especially after the 2016 election, to be a credible backer of a digital currency. True to Zuckerberg's famous aphorism—"Move fast and break things"—the company had moved fast in using the personal data of its users. And it had broken its reputation in the process.

That said, a private digital currency could offer significant advantages to companies like Netflix and ESPN. Companies like AT&T and Microsoft already allow their customers to pay in crypto through payments processors like BitPay. It doesn't really matter why they have opted to do so: because it sounds cool, because their customers have a philosophical commitment to crypto, or because of privacy concerns. All that matters is that customers seem to want the option. A more stable digital currency would be more appealing to large companies. It might even allow them to expand into other product lines: for example, ESPN might offer sports betting, something it has already shown an interest in, though such undertakings would have regulatory complications.[55]

Even if some of these companies balked at accepting the leadership of Amazon, a competitor, all of them would understand that the power to control money in the United States—and perhaps elsewhere—would create an extraordinary pool of economic rents. There would be more than enough of those rents to go around, even if Amazon got the largest share.

That is decidedly not to say that a private digital currency would create *social* value. Indeed, it would create complex problems involving tax avoidance, monetary policy, illicit activity, and more. But the challenge confronting the United States government is that maintaining the status quo looks difficult, and it might need to make a preemptive move to a central bank digital currency in order to prevent the establishment of a private digital currency that competes with the dollar.

Pillar 3 is regulatory. Amazon would acknowledge that by issuing amazons it would effectively be acting as a money-market mutual fund. So the company would readily agree to have its currency operation regulated by the Securities and Exchange Commission as a money-market fund (MMF). MMFs are subject to what's known as Rule 2a-7 of the Investment Company Act of 1940. That rule specifies a number of conditions about how an MMF's portfolio can be invested, including the credit quality of assets in which an MMF can invest, how diversified the portfolio must be, how liquid it must be, and the maturity structure of the assets held.[56] Amazon could agree to meet or exceed all these conditions and commit to making its digital currency reserve the squeakiest of squeaky-clean money-market funds.

If Amazon started to expand into other financial services, such as offering credit products to sellers on its platform, then there would be other regulations with which it would need to comply. But the main game for Amazon would be creating a dominant private digital currency, not trying to make money or skirt regulations related to banking operations. So it could, in this domain, act completely in good faith while pursuing the objective of getting the network-externality flywheel spinning to expand the use of its digital currency.

Regulatory compliance also would allow amazons to have the stable-coin features that were at the heart of the libra model. Instead of the Libra Reserve, there would be the Amazon Reserve. Keeping its entire reserve in US government securities would satisfy regulatory requirements and also give amazon holders confidence that they could exchange them for US dollars (or other currencies, since Amazon is a global business) on demand.[57] Amazon would essentially run a money-market fund in each of the currencies with which it offered convertibility. This would be an advantage for international consumers who wanted to avoid exchange-rate risk. Moreover, it would arguably give holders of amazons greater faith that there would not be a modern-day bank run on amazons, because convertibility into local currencies would reduce the risk of exchange-rate hedging by customers.

Pillar 4 is financial inclusion. Libra painted a compelling picture of the plight of those excluded from banking—not only in sub-Saharan Africa but also in South Central Los Angeles and the South Side of Chicago. Many people in these communities have no bank account or else pay extremely high fees for access to ATMs and other basic banking services. Lacking other options, they may pay exorbitant interest rates on payday loans. Part of the pitch for a private digital currency could be offering people in these communities access to cheap, secure financial services. While doing so might not be profitable for existing banks and financial services companies, a company like Amazon could easily absorb the cost as a kind of loss leader.

Elements of this idea bear a relationship to an initially underappreciated benefit of blockchain technology—the financial innovation known as initial coin offerings (ICOs).[58] ICOs are a novel financial use of so-called tokens, or coins, issued on a blockchain ledger to raise money for blockchain investments. Tokenization permits the creation of a range of financial instruments, some new and some simply better, that have great potential in financial markets.

To see how this works, let's start with Filecoin, which raised $257 million in 2017 in its ICO.[59] The purpose of the underlying enterprise was to set up a data-storage market. Both buyers and sellers would have to use FIL tokens for transactions. Filecoin promised to issue a maximum of 200 million FIL tokens.[60] So, in principle, the total value of all FIL tokens would be equal to the revenue generated in that part of the disk-storage market. The value of a single token is this revenue divided by the number of tokens. The owner of a FIL token is essentially buying a security connected to (or "making a bet" on) revenue in the data-storage market. The holder of such a security can resell it to people who want to buy storage on the network. In the ICO 10 percent of the tokens were sold to investors, so the total valuation of Filecoin's future revenues was $2.57 billion.[61]

Amazon is not the only company that might be able to create a private digital currency that largely supplants the US dollar. Google is another company with a huge base of both consumer and business users. Apple is another obvious example.

Before we look at how the US government could head off this challenge to the control of money by creating its own digital currency, it's important to understand the challenges involved in regulating cryptocurrencies, as well as the environmental issues raised by the (currently) most popular consensus protocol for those currencies.

REGULATING CRYPTO

One threat of cryptocurrencies is their use for tax evasion. This is, in principle, remarkably easy. Anup Malani and I outlined a scheme for doing so in a 2018 *New York Times* opinion piece.

> Suppose A, B and C are electronic addresses you own. You let the I.R.S. [Internal Revenue Service] know you own A, but not B and C. You buy one Bitcoin at $15,000 and park it at A, expecting the price to go up. Just a few hours later, when a Bitcoin is worth $15,500, you send that Bitcoin to B and then to C. . . . A few months later, when your Bitcoin is now worth $25,000, you send it from C to A and tell the I.R.S., "I sold a Bitcoin to an anonymous counterparty at B back at $15,500 and just now bought a Bitcoin from another anonymous counterparty at C for $25,000." As a result, you owe taxes on capital gains of just $500 rather than $10,000.[62]

Of course, bitcoin might not go up in value, but tax evasion is relevant only if you make money. If you lose money, you can just reveal this loss to the IRS and claim a deduction against other income or accumulate the loss to offset against future income. This scheme succeeds simply because the IRS does not know the true identity of the owner of the three addresses. As we noted in our article, "The I.R.S. can observe all the transactions between A, B and C on the bitcoin blockchain, but it cannot disprove that B and C are 'arm's length' counterparties (that is, independent and not colluding). Rules in the United States that require financial institutions to verify the identity of address holders do not solve the problem, because as far as the I.R.S. knows, B and C could have been set up by a foreign institution that does not comply with such rules."[63] This is a cautionary tale, but it also suggests how tax authorities can defeat this kind of scheme.

Another concern about cryptocurrencies is their use to facilitate trade in illicit goods. Just like tax evasion, the use of cryptocurrency for illicit activity relies—or at least leans heavily—on the anonymity of the account holder. When a centralized authority—such as a bank or other financial institution—is aware of such activity, they can be pressured by relevant authorities to reveal the identity of the account holder. For years, Swiss banks famously kept the identity of account holders secret, allowing foreign nationals to evade taxes by parking money in Swiss bank accounts. This practice began to unravel in 2009, when the US Department of Justice began charging Swiss banking professionals themselves with crimes. In 2012 the DOJ indicted Switzerland's oldest bank (a bank that had branches only in Switzerland) on charges of conspiracy to evade taxes, and in 2013 the bank pleaded guilty.[64] Eventually the Swiss government began cooperating with the DOJ, and the IRS began to offer a voluntary disclosure program that effectively required Swiss banks to report on each other.[65]

Without a bank or other institution that knows the identity of its account holders, the only information the authorities have for tracing financial activity is a string of numbers. And because of the decentralized nature of the blockchain, there's effectively nothing they can do about transfers to and from an account. There is, however, one pinch point: where cryptocurrency is converted to or from fiat currency. If you wanted to buy bitcoin with dollars, you would probably go through an exchange like Swyftx. "Know your customer" or KYC-1 rules require such exchanges to record the identity of people wanting to withdraw or deposit dollars through the exchange with an identification document like a driver's license. When illegal activity is suspected, a court may issue a subpoena to force a crypto exchange to divulge the identity of an account holder. For instance, in late 2017, the IRS successfully petitioned a US federal judge to order the popular cryptocurrency exchange Coinbase to reveal the identity of more than fourteen thousand account holders suspected of involvement in illicit activity. But such legal measures are premised on the exchange's actually knowing the identity of the account holders. In practice, it is not a simple or mechanical task for authorities to obtain this information.

In general, these rules, and focusing on large on- and off-ramping transactions, help regulators cut down on the use of cryptocurrency for illicit activities. If you suddenly deposit $200 million in your Bank of America account, that transaction gets noticed. And US authorities have powers to seize those assets based on reasonable suspicions about their provenance. But in a world where cryptocurrencies can be used to buy a wide range of goods and services, things are much more complicated for regulators. The seizure of assets such as $400 million superyachts belonging to Russian oligarchs suggests that it is difficult even for the powerful to evade international regulatory efforts. But these incidents also highlight the difficulties faced by regulators. Focusing on a small number of extremely wealthy, well-known people can be quite successful in capturing the proceeds of illicit activities. But doing this on a wider scale is inherently problematic. How would the IRS or any other agency manage to track down the Ford F-150 Lightning of every—or any—small-time methamphetamine dealer?

Alternatively, one might imagine trying to make the purchases of goods or services with cryptocurrency the pinch point. But this approach has its own problems, not least that it would turn every business into an IRS enforcement agent. There are some important clues here, however, for the design of a govcoin. If the wallet used to make transactions in the digital currency were subject to a KYC rule, then a transaction in cryptocurrency could be traced in the same way as a credit card transaction.

Such a govcoin would differ significantly from cash because it would lack the anonymity that cash affords. This anonymity is why many jurisdictions have anti-money-laundering rules that require cash transactions above a certain amount—say $10,000—to be traced. And it's part of why India's bungled attempt to crack down on illegal activity involved getting rid of the two highest-denomination banknotes, which offered both portability and anonymity.

One of the common criticisms of current cryptocurrencies, like bitcoin, is that they can't be used to buy many things. That is a blessing for regulators, at least for now. If a private digital currency became widely used for everyday transactions, then it would be almost impossible for regulators to ferret out ill-gotten gains.

Another headache for regulators is the use of cryptocurrency as a speculative and largely unregulated investment. This issue began to attract more attention in early to mid-2022, as the crypto crash began to affect "ordinary" investors. Previously, bitcoin and other cryptocurrencies were the province of crypto enthusiasts and a few wealthy investors like the Winklevoss twins (of *The Social Network* fame). But by 2022, as the total market value of cryptocurrencies pushed past $3 trillion, the crypto craze had spread to people who, on the whole, didn't understand the risks they were taking by investing in crypto and were sometimes not able to afford the losses that ensued.

Paul Krugman framed these issues starkly in his *New York Times* column: "Investors in crypto seem to be different from investors in other risky assets, like stocks, who consist disproportionately of affluent, college-educated whites. According to a survey by the research organization NORC, 44 percent of crypto investors are nonwhite, and 55 percent don't have a college degree. . . . NORC says that this is great, that 'cryptocurrencies are opening up investing opportunities for more diverse investors.' But I remember the days when subprime mortgage lending was similarly celebrated—when it was hailed as a way to open up the benefits of homeownership to previously excluded groups."[66]

This trend presents regulators with a dilemma. The liberal perspective that has been the animating principle of financial regulation in most advanced economies is that people should be free to choose—even if they end up making bad choices. This principle is tempered by another—that people should not be defrauded. And the line between being free to make a bad choice and being taken advantage of by an unscrupulous counterparty is, in practice, a pretty blurry one.

On top of this, there are risks to financial stability even if reasonably well-informed investors are taking risks that they see as rational. In the hyperconnected world in which we live, their risk-taking behavior can adversely affect others. No investor is an island. During the 2008 financial crisis, investment banks that were highly leveraged and invested in various securities connected to subprime loans and other mortgages got themselves into serious trouble: Bears Sterns and Lehman Brothers bankrupted themselves. But the trouble wasn't limited to those firms. There were disastrous ripple effects throughout the US and global financial systems that required a great deal of hard work and a large dose of good look to avoid a repeat of the Great Depression.

The unique problem with cryptocurrency is that it's completely unclear whom to regulate. It's easy to find the issuer of a corporate bond or mortgage-backed security. But who is the "issuer" of bitcoin? In July 2022, Lael Brainard, vice chair of the US Federal Reserve, observed that "the crypto financial system turns out to be susceptible to the same risks that are all too familiar from traditional finance, such as leverage, settlement, opacity, and maturity and liquidity transformation."[67] Brainard also pointed to a number of shortcomings—most already well understood—of crypto assets. The list is a useful road map for thinking about how a private digital currency along the lines suggested in this chapter would be able to supplant existing cryptocurrencies such as bitcoin. Brainard listed three issues:

1. Crypto assets as currently constituted are very volatile. Bitcoin lost 60 percent of its value between April and June 2022.
2. The existing generation of stable coins is not immune to the kind of crises of confidence that noncrypto assets are. As Brainard put it, "New technology and financial engineering cannot by themselves convert risky assets into safe ones." If the venerable Reserve Primary Fund could break the buck in 2008, and a Wall Street icon like Goldman Sachs could nearly go to the wall even when it was on the right side of bets on mortgage-backed-securities, it's not surprising that a stable coin like terra could be subject to a modern-day bank run.
3. Related to this, Brainard observed that "crypto platforms are highly vulnerable to deleveraging, fire sales, and contagion—risks that are well known from traditional finance."[68]

Brainard went on to argue that assets that pose the same risk should be subject to the same regulatory framework—but this fails to engage with the question of how to do that. One avenue is by monitoring conversion transactions, as discussed above. Another is regulating the involvement of existing financial institutions, such as banks. But this is a somewhat old-school view of digital assets. Regulators need to engage with the reality of fully decentralized cryptocurrencies and related assets and recognize that even though the risks they pose may be similar to those of nondigital assets, fewer tools are available to manage those risks.

Brainard did acknowledge the possible benefits of a central bank digital currency that "could enhance stability by providing the neutral trusted settlement layer in the future crypto financial system. . . . This development would be a natural evolution of the complementarity between the public and private sectors in payments, ensuring strong public trust in the one-for-one redeemability of commercial bank money and stable coins for safe central bank money." But again she returned to the theme that if a digital asset walks like a duck and talks like a duck, then it should be regulated like a duck, saying "it is vital that stable coins that purport to be redeemable at par in fiat currency on demand are subject to the types of prudential regulation that limit the risk of runs and payment system vulnerabilities that such private monies have exhibited historically." Sure, sure. But how?[69]

Brainard's remarks were—perhaps not surprisingly—consistent with a report from the President's Working Group on Financial Markets. Its three main recommendations were that stable-coin issuers should be insured depository institutions, just as banks are under the FDIC; that custodial wallet providers should be subject to federal regulation to address concerns about "payment system risk"; and that stable-coin issuers should have limited connections with commercial entities. This last point seems to pick up on the idea that a big player like Amazon, Google, or Apple could encourage consumers away from dollars and toward their stable coin, thereby kickstarting the network-externality flywheel. The report even proposed forced interoperability between stable coins and "limits on affiliation with commercial entities or on use of users' transaction data."[70] These are classic antitrust remedies that have been discussed extensively in the context of digital markets. These are good ideas: the question is how one can do that in a world of decentralized, anonymous crypto. In other words: Sure, sure. But how?

The answer I outline in the next chapter is that central banks need to crowd out private digital currencies by issuing their own "govcoin." Such a currency must provide most of the benefits that private digital currencies offer while withdrawing the one critical feature that facilitates illicit activity—pure anonymity. At the same time, a govcoin needs to provide enough anonymity to permit the (legitimate) full-functionality kind of smart contracts that that Web3 would make possible.

This is a narrow path, but one which can be navigated. And it is a path on which governments around the world have already embarked. The US government is late to the race but can still win it. It is vital for the functioning of the global financial system that it do so. In fact, it is critical for US sovereign power, with implications that go well beyond the world of money and finance, as I discuss in chapter 6.

WHAT ABOUT THE PLANET?

A frequently voiced concern about cryptocurrency is the amount of computational time and energy it consumes. The bitcoin network uses eighty terawatt-hours (TWh) of electricity a year. That's a lot, and, if there is little value to bitcoin, then the environmental and social costs it incurs are wasteful.

But how do we calculate that cost? Using the latest, most highly regarded estimate of the social cost of carbon as $125 per ton and using the Environmental Protection Agency's (EPA) conversion rate of 4.33×10^{-4} metric tons of carbon produced per kilowatt-hour (kWh) of electricity generated, we arrive at a social cost of approximately $4.3 billion a year.[71] But the amount of energy consumed varies depending on the price of bitcoin. The Cambridge Bitcoin Electricity Consumption Index acknowledges that the amount could be more like 150 TWh a year, which would put the annual social cost of bitcoin at $8.1 billion.[72] And bitcoin isn't the only blockchain network in the world, so the total social cost may be around $15–20 billion a year. And if a proof-of-work consensus protocol drove *all* the currency in the world, in the wake of a transition from traditional fiat currencies to private digital currencies like libra, it would consume a colossal amount of energy and incur a breathtakingly large social cost.

Of course, such a scheme would be politically nonviable, which is partly why the Libra white paper proposed using a proof-of-stake, not proof-of-work, protocol. Essentially, instead of using the solving of cryptographic problems as a means of validating blocks, POS uses a process known as *voting for validation*. Roughly speaking, nodes in a POS blockchain bet coins that the transaction they are validating actually occurred. If other nodes "outbet" them, by staking more coins to assert that the transaction did not occur, then the original bet is lost.[73]

As of mid-2022, Buterin's brainchild, Ethereum, like bitcoin, used a POW consensus protocol. But Buterin had long intended to switch to POS, which could reduce the Ethereum network's energy consumption by as much as 99.95 percent.[74] This switch from POW to POS—known as "the merge"—was mooted for years until Buterin gave assurances that it would finally occur in August 2022. And, indeed, it did.

Pulling off the merge was the sort of thing that could only be done by someone with Buterin's unique status in the Ethereum community. It is an example of a big, high-stakes coordination problem—like Sweden deciding to switch the side of the road on which people drove. It requires planning, getting the buy-in of the community, and thinking carefully about what could go wrong and how to remedy problems. Above all, it requires people believing that it's going to happen and believing that others believe it's going to happen—what economists call "higher-order beliefs." A central network actor like Buterin coordinates people's higher-order beliefs.[75]

5

GOVCOINS

THUS FAR I'VE PAINTED A PICTURE digital money as having two main attributes. First, it allows users to do some things that they can't do easily, or at all, with physical cash. A platform like Ethereum allows users to write smart contracts that—at least in principle—increase economic efficiency by mitigating hold-up problems. Second, the issuer of the main medium of exchange in an economy holds huge power. And which currency is the dominant medium of exchange is a coordination game—just like deciding which side of the road we drive on. A private organization wanting to seize power from the US government might be able to do so if they could get folks to coordinate on their currency rather than the US dollar.

It's fair to say that the United States has been slow to recognize this, and they're behind the race with other countries. But that's the topic of the next chapter. For now, we're going to focus on the race between the US government and the private sector. This is a race in which—thanks to Janet Yellen—the United States is in a strong position. Early in her tenure as treasury secretary she put a stop to Facebook's proposal to create a digital currency, and in early 2022 she began outlining a path toward a US govcoin.

In her April 2022 speech at American University, Yellen outlined the elements of such a path. But the most important part of her speech was what we might call the Yellen Doctrine: "Sovereign money is the core of a well-functioning financial system, and the US benefits from the central role the dollar and US financial institutions play in global finance."[1]

She followed this observation with a lesson about what happened when the United States did not have a uniform national currency— what the first occupant of her office, Alexander Hamilton, described as "immense disorder." Even in the mid-nineteenth century the United States had a fragmented monetary system. Banks in different states issued their own banknotes; they could be used elsewhere and exchanged, but with significant transaction costs. And although President Abraham Lincoln made some progress toward a national currency with the National Bank Act, it was the Federal Reserve Act of 1913 that finally provided a unified national currency.

We often speak of the twentieth century as "the American century." While Britain, France, and Germany gave away power in acts of self-harm and the Soviet Union pursued an economically flawed system, America's population and economy grew strongly. The United States helped create, and then supported, the core institutions of the postwar international order. America became the cradle of innovation in the postwar manufacturing era and even more so in the digital age. The strength and stability of the US dollar played a pivotal role in the country's global dominance. To sustain that strength in the future, the United States needs to implement a central bank digital currency.

DESIGNING A US GOVCOIN

What would a US central bank digital currency look like? There are numerous choices here. It should have as many of the benefits of private digital currencies as possible without some of the key drawbacks. The first major choice is whether the govcoin would be a *retail* or *wholesale* central bank digital currency, or some combination of the two.

A retail govcoin would be a digital currency provided by the central bank directly to the public. The world's first govcoin was the Bahamian sand dollar (BSD), launched in October 2020. The BSD was the result of a collaboration between the Central Bank of the Bahamas and Mastercard. The public could instantly convert between BSD and Bahamian dollars through a digital wallet available on their smartphones through an app called Island Pay. The app could be used for purchases in stores, for taxis, to top up prepaid mobile phone accounts, and to send money to other users.[2] In a country comprising seven hundred small islands in five thousand square miles of ocean, it's easy to see why this technology would be valuable. The cash distribution, handling, and processing frictions that I discussed in chapter 2 loom particularly large in the Bahamas.

But *mobile* money is not the same as *digital* money. For many purposes, a tap card could work just as well as the BSD and Island Pay. Both systems use basically identical near-field communication technology. Apple Pay and Google Pay provide consumers with precisely the same functionality as the Bahamian govcoin linked to the Island Pay app. One obvious benefit of such a technology is that, using point-of-sale equipment, merchants can accept app payments in a country that doesn't have the same digital payments infrastructure as, say, Sweden. However, the Bahamian approach has a significant drawback relative to existing tap cards: it is prepaid. That is, consumers have to load money (for instance, from a bank account) onto the Island Pay app before they can use it for purchases. Having to constantly transfer money from a bank account (or a less convenient and more costly source) is clearly less efficient than a Swedish-style payments system.

This is useful innovation, but it has relatively little to do with a central bank digital currency, except that it involved the Bahamian Central Bank. At its heart, this initiative was really about rolling out a digital-payments infrastructure. It has had positive benefits for financial inclusion, but it is more about mobile money than digital money.

A different approach to creating a govcoin is a *wholesale* central bank digital currency (CBDC). A number of countries are currently exploring this approach, including Hong Kong, Singapore, and Thailand. A significant feature of these systems is the facilitation of cross-border payments. These typically take several days, impose nontrivial transaction costs, and may also involve liquidity and credit risks. A wholesale CBDC provides a new payments infrastructure for interbank settlements by using blockchain technology.

A good example of what this might look like is the mBridge project, a collaboration between the Bank for International Settlements, the Hong Kong Monetary Authority, the Bank of Thailand, the Digital Currency Institute of the People's Bank of China, and the Central Bank of the United Arab Emirates. A joint report issued by these central banks in late 2021 noted that the "common prototype platform for mCBDC settlements was able to complete international transfers and foreign exchange operations in seconds, as opposed to the several days normally required for any transaction to be completed using the existing network of commercial banks, and operate on a 24/7 basis."[3] The report claimed that the transaction costs to users could be cut by half. This sounds like exactly the sort of technology-driven innovation that improves the international flow of money and leads to a more efficient allocation of resources. Given that many people in lower-income countries depend financially on remittances from relatives working in higher-income countries, more efficient international monetary transfers also enhance economic equality and development.

Anyone who has sent money from the United States to the United Kingdom or Australia (or vice versa) knows how slow and expensive international funds transfers can be. This is largely because there are basically no multilateral solutions for these cross-border payments. Transfers are made through a network of banks known as "correspondent banks." These banks act as stepping stones by which payments hop from a bank in one country to a bank in another. It's easy to see how this creates frictions in moving money. Those frictions are exacerbated by the fact that these banks are in different time zones and don't operate around the clock. This is magnified further by regulatory requirements such as KYC rules and anti-money-laundering provisions—all of which are important but often result in duplication of effort by multiple banks. And, as a kicker, given that this all takes time and exchange rates move up and down—these markets don't sleep—there is foreign exchange risk exposure throughout the process.

Whereas the current process takes three to five days, the mBridge process claims to complete transfers in two to ten seconds. The system uses a form of blockchain technology in which the validation function is permissioned. Unlike Bitcoin or Ethereum, in which anybody can be a node, the mBridge distributed ledger allows only central banks or other trusted parties to be nodes. As the report emphasizes: "Having trusted validators reduces the computational resources necessary to securely validate transactions."[4] A restricted set of parties—basically commercial banks—could submit transactions to be verified and added to the ledger, and financial technology and other firms could be given permission to view the ledger.

Using wholesale govcoins for these cross-border transactions connects commercial banks in different countries in a way that facilitates rapid settlement. The settlement mechanism used, known as *payment versus payment* (PvP), ensures that the eventual transfer of a payment in (say) govcoin A happens if and only if the final transfer of payment in govcoin B occurs. Smart contracts are at the heart of automating this process, and it depends on "tokenizing" the different govcoins into a common medium of exchange (for example, an ERC-20 token).

Although this process is efficient, a number of questions and drawbacks remain. The mBridge system does not allow for fully atomic transactions, or what in blockchain parlance is a genuine "atomic swap" (an automated contract that allows two parties to trade tokens from two different blockchains). No one jurisdiction can view the balance of all pending transactions, and "an optimal liquidity savings mechanism has yet to be found."[5]

The current proposals also raise questions about the ability of the international community to enforce sanctions on individuals, corporations, or countries. This issue is particularly salient at present given the war between Russia and Ukraine and the international community's quite effective use of sanctions through the existing international financial network. Some of these sanctions have involved individual countries banning imports, such as oil and gas from Russia. Other sanctions have been driven by consumer expectations, which have placed pressure on companies across almost all sectors of the economy to stop doing business (in one form or another) in Russia.[6]

Sanctions involving the international financial system have been largely coordinated through SWIFT, the international financial messaging service. SWIFT is a cooperative founded in 1973. Its members include around eleven thousand banks and other financial institutions in two hundred countries. Oversight of SWIFT is provided by the central banks of the G10 economies. Because it is incorporated in Belgium, its conduct is governed by Belgian law and European Union regulations. Under this governance, SWIFT can disconnect certain banks from the network at certain times, putting a halt to their international transactions. It did this in March 2012 pursuant to EU Regulation 267/2012, which prohibited SWIFT (and other financial messaging companies) from providing services to EU-sanctioned banks in Iran. In March 2022, under a series of EU regulations, messaging providers such as SWIFT were prohibited from providing services to seven Russian and three Belarusian entities.[7]

It's unclear whether a widespread move to wholesale central bank digital currencies would permit the same degree of international coordination in imposing sanctions. The answer could depend on details such as the precise nature of the consensus protocol. Without getting mired in the details, mBridge uses a Byzantine fault tolerance consensus protocol built on the Ethereum blockchain model, although it is a permissioned blockchain. This leaves open the question of whether transfers between banks in countries subject to international sanctions could be verified on the ledger. In principle, a CBDC—such as an e-ruble, if it existed—could be excluded from the network. But this would certainly be trickier than simply informing SWIFT that Belgian law requires it to cut off certain Russian banks. These considerations will loom large as the politics of govcoins evolves.

International funds transfers are important, but the main game for a wholesale govcoin is within a particular country. A central bank like the US Federal Reserve might consider a retail govcoin, a wholesale govcoin, or some kind of hybrid model. Each model has different implications for the functioning of the banking system.

Under a *wholesale* CBDC model, the Fed would use blockchain technology for settlement between commercial banks and the Fed. The existing banking system would be left intact in the sense that currency issued by a commercial bank would still be a claim against the bank, not the Fed. Blockchain technology would increase efficiency of the settlement process in a manner similar to that proposed by mBridge for foreign exchange transactions. But, since the settlement frictions within the United States are smaller than those across borders, the efficiency gains per transaction would be correspondingly smaller. On the other hand, settlement volumes are dramatically larger within the United States, so the overall benefit could still be large.

Under a *direct retail* CBDC model, the Fed would handle all retail payments and maintain a ledger. This would mean that there was no longer any need for retail banks, and the Fed would be responsible for some existing bank functions, like providing accounts and enforcing KYC rules.

Under an *intermediated retail* CBDC model, the Fed would deal only with wholesale balances between commercial banks and would not have any direct role in retail transactions. Under a *hybrid retail* CBDC model, the Fed would leave customer-facing activities to commercial banks but would maintain the ledger of balances.

Fedcoin

Rather than go through the pros and cons of each of these models, I'm going to propose a specific model for the Fed's govcoin (which I'm calling *fedcoin*) and then explore its strengths and weaknesses. I base my proposal on several principles.

I. CUSTOMER COMPETITION

The banking system involves customer-facing activities in which the Federal Reserve is currently not involved and in which the public benefits from competition among providers. My first principle is that competition and consumer choice are valuable ends in themselves and that competition in the customer-facing aspects of retail banking should be preserved. Right now, that means preserving retail banking by not having the Fed competing directly with banks on the customer side.

In an environment where retail banks and payments companies like Square compete to provide terminals to merchants, and where customers need only a mobile phone to make payments, retail banks are unlikely to earn significant revenues from being involved in these activities. Yet those financial institutions will still hold deposits and have relationships with customers. These financial institutions will thus have access to valuable data about their customers, such as spending patterns and account balances. This information can give these institutions advantages in providing loans and other financial products to customers. In addition, this approach preserves the great social value of customers' having ownership over their personal financial data and being able to switch easily between retail banks.

Such arrangements are sometimes called *open banking*. This is related to the idea of giving customers the ability to keep their mobile phone number when switching between telecommunications providers. Retail banks, like phone companies, should be prevented from erecting artificial barriers that make it costly and time-consuming for customers to switch providers. The ability to switch gives customers more bargaining power and reduces the fees and charges that a bank can extract from them.

2. FEDCOIN AS THE BACKBONE OF WEB3

To fend off the threats of a private digital currency, fedcoin would need to have much of the same functionality. It should emulate what Ethereum achieved by having a Turing-complete programming language and digital currency on a single platform. Indeed, because Ethereum is based on open-source code, it is replicable in a technical sense. But in order for fedcoin to take the place of ether, it would have to adopt a token-based rather than an account-based approach.

The difference between these two approaches has been much debated in CBDC pilot programs. Although somewhat semantic, it is important.[8] Tokens are what is known as *bearer instruments*. They entitle the person who holds them to something of a certain monetary value. Banknotes are a bearer instrument. By contrast, an account-based approach to fedcoin would involve a monetary balance in an account at a retail bank.

Tokens and accounts differ in their means of verification. Tokens are verified by the receiver, whereas for accounts, an intermediary is required to verify the identity of the account holder. For instance, a payment from a traditional bank account is deemed to be valid if the bank confirms that the person making the payment is, in fact, the account holder and not some other party. If the bank makes an error in this verification task, then the bank has to return the funds to the true account holder. Under a token-based system, what has to be verified is the authenticity of the token itself.

Tokens, since they are bearer instruments, create the potential for double spending. Satoshi Nakamoto's great innovation was developing a way to prevent double spending of tokens using a decentralized ledger. A tokenized fedcoin would likewise involve all transactions being recorded in a ledger. In principle, that ledger need not be centralized (i.e., held solely by the Federal Reserve).

Such a ledger would provide a record of which fedcoins have been used by which account holders. This is no different from a credit or debit card, but it is less anonymous than cash. Some of the efficiencies of a digital currency, such as the avoidance of hold-up problems, arise from the smart contracts that make use of anonymity to prevent renegotiation. These efficiencies could still be achieved with a tokenized fedcoin, even with KYC rules. Knowledge of the real-world identity of a customer could be walled off from smart contracts and even from aspects of the legal system by statute. The true identity of customers could thus be used to track and prevent the use of fedcoins for illicit activities such as trade in illegal goods and tax evasion while still permitting the full functionality of smart contracts.

Tokenized fedcoins would allow for other mundane but very valuable uses of smart money and smart contracts. For instance, actual exchanges of fedcoin could be made conditional on the satisfaction of certain conditions. This is important in the simultaneous exchange of currencies (PvP exchanges) and in mitigating the risks that come with the transaction not occurring as planned (known as *Herstatt risk*). This functionality is also useful in securities trading, which relies on the simultaneous exchange of a security and the "liquidity leg" (known as *delivery versus payment* exchanges). In fact, this problem arises in *all* spot contracting. I hand over payment of one form or another, and a coffee-shop owner hands me a skim latte. You hand me a cashier's check, and I give you the keys to the car I am selling you. Some of these exchanges are backed by legal rules about theft or fraud, as well as by social norms. But this raises an intriguing question: how much mutually beneficial spot contracting doesn't occur because of exchange risk? This type of risk can be avoided using a tokenized fedcoin together with smart-money or smart-contracting apps.

Of course, people have been grappling for a long time with the problems of guaranteeing secure exchanges for important trades, like securities. Trades can be made securely through a trusted third party. (If that were not the case, we wouldn't have a stock market!) In securities trading this is known as a "central securities depository," and in foreign exchange as "continuous linked settlement." But the involvement of third parties creates frictions. Decentralized finance—or DeFi—has introduced alternative mechanisms using innovations such as distributed ledgers and tokenized payments. A suitably designed fedcoin could help foster such innovation while eliminating much of the rationale for an alternative, purely private-sector solution.

3. A CENTRALIZED LEDGER

A core consideration in the design of a govcoin is whether the central bank maintains a centralized ledger. It is certainly possible to have a tokenized govcoin with a decentralized ledger. Indeed, Sweden has piloted such an approach with its e-krona.[9] Two important questions are whether there is a single core ledger of transactions that is owned by the central bank, and whether the central bank has a direct contractual relationship with the end user of the govcoin. Maintaining a core ledger would mean that the Fed would not need cooperation from retail banks in order to take action against bank customers engaged in illicit activities. This might sound like a moot point when it comes to US banks, which would already be strongly inclined to cooperate. But it could become far more problematic if illicit activities were being conducted through nonbank institutions or a fully private digital currency.

Under my proposal, the US Federal Reserve would provide a core ledger. All fedcoin holders would have digital wallets in which all transactions would be recorded.

4. INTERNATIONAL NEUTRALITY

While it is reasonable for the United States to create a fedcoin and seek to maintain its status as the global reserve currency, doing so should not lead to the loss of monetary authority for other countries. This could be avoided with one important feature of the fedcoin.

Imagine that fedcoin became a popular medium of exchange in Japan and showed signs of displacing the yen in a significant portion of the Japanese economy. It would be hard for Japanese authorities to enforce a law barring the use of the digital currency and saying that the yen was the only currency that could be used in Japan. The widespread use of fedcoin would make it borderline impossible for the Bank of Japan to set interest rates in the country.

This could be prevented, however, by the United States' allowing commercial banks to issue fedcoin wallets only to US nationals. That way, no Japanese citizen could have a fedcoin wallet and use the coin in Japan. Foreign travelers needing to use fedcoin in the United States could be issued with time-limited wallets that could be filled only with transferred foreign currency (like yen).

An alternative would be to have the fedcoin digital wallet be region coded, so that it could be used only in the United States and its territories. Either way, an international treaty to ensure that all countries maintained monetary sovereignty would be important for the legitimacy of fedcoin, to prevent the United States from imposing potentially large costs on other countries.

THE IMPACT ON US MONETARY POLICY

How would a central bank digital currency—either wholesale or resale—affect the way the Fed controls short-term interest rates?

As chapter 3 explains, the key short-term interest rate in the US economy is the federal funds rate, which is based on the price of the funds needed by banks to meet the reserve requirements imposed by the Fed in order for banks to make payments to customers. The way the Fed uses the supply of reserves to set the federal funds rate is known as the *ample reserves regime*. In contrast to the way the Fed controlled interest rates before the 2008 financial crisis, it now does so mainly by setting the rate it pays on bank reserves, rather than by actively managing the supply of reserves. By controlling the amount it pays banks on excess reserves, the Fed creates a floor on the rate at which banks are willing to lend to each other in the overnight market, because they could always just leave the money in their own reserve account and earn the same rate. And the Fed can lend directly to banks through the discount window, whereby banks post assets as collateral. The rate at the discount window acts as a ceiling for the federal funds rate. The Fed can then squeeze the floor and ceiling together to achieve the Federal Funds Rate it wants.

The seemingly small difference between account-based money and token-based money has important consequences for the ample reserves regime and the way the Fed controls short-term interest rates. Traditional bank deposits—being account-based—are a claim on the assets of the issuing bank. If the account holder wants her money back, she has recourse to the bank's balance sheet. This is why bank deposits are sometimes referred to as *inside money*. But some tokenized forms of money are also inside money. For instance, tokens from the popular Chinese financial services company Alipay are also inside money. Because they are tokenized forms of money, all that has to be verified is the authenticity of the token. Ultimately those tokens are a claim on Alipay's balance sheet.

By contrast, government-issued fiat money like the US dollar or Japanese yen is known as *outside money* because it does not represent a claim on the balance sheet of the issuer—at least not in the traditional sense. What can I do if I want to "redeem" my US dollars? During the gold standard era I could demand, at least in principle, that the US government redeem my dollars for gold. After August 15, 1971, when President Richard Nixon took the US off the gold standard, that was no longer possible. All I can really cause the US government to do with US dollars today is offset any US tax obligations.

It's useful to distinguish, then, between *central bank money* (which is a liability of the Fed) and *commercial bank money* (which is a liability of a particular commercial bank). At the end of 2021 there was about $6.4 trillion in central bank money in the United States. Of that amount, $2.2 trillion was cash circulating in the economy, and $4.2 trillion was held in (digital) reserves at the Fed. The volume of commercial bank money was greater: $18.2 trillion in deposits. These funds were used to provide credit of $16.4 trillion in loans of one form or another to households, businesses, and governments.[10]

How do commercial banks "create" money? In the practice known as *fractional reserve banking*, commercial banks create their own deposit liabilities by crediting the accounts of borrowers (i.e., customers to whom the bank lends) with the funds the bank lends to them. So, when the bank makes a loan, it records a new asset (the loan) and a new liability (the deposit).

Pure financial intermediaries do not create money, even though they make loans. Intermediaries lend money that already exists. They accept funds from customers and lend those funds out.

My model for fedcoin differs from the current financial system in an important way. In order to have a centralized ledger and tokenized money, the Fed would take on a greater role in the creation of credit. In a sense, commercial banks would perform all the functions they do today *except* creating credit. In a sense, they would be financial intermediaries.

In one hypothetical scenario, fedcoin would not pay interest directly to end users. Instead, banks holding accounts with the Fed would earn interest on reserves, just as they do today. The difference would be that those reserves would be denominated in fedcoin rather than US dollars. Banks would make electronic deposits into their reserve accounts with the Fed, using fedcoin. The ledger on which these transactions are recorded would be on a blockchain rather than the current ledger, but that would really just be a detail from the perspective of the banks.

This wouldn't work—or at least it might not work well—because it would violate design principle 2, that fedcoin should be the backbone of Web3. Having banks create credit in a tokenized system would effectively require them to create their own coins, which would represent a claim on the assets of the bank in question. Those coins would then have to be convertible one-for-one into fedcoin, and smart contracts would have to be denominated in fedcoin. The Fed would also need to maintain the centralized ledger to prevent digital money being used for illicit activities. These requirements would involve an inherent clash between the private coins being used by individual banks to create credit and the centralized ledger run by the Fed.

If banks ceased to create credit and focused purely on interfacing with customers, the shift would have large implications for the mechanics of conducting monetary policy. It would amount to a swap of the central bank digital currency for deposits. But this substitution would simply change the composition of bank funding, not the level of it, at least—as the economists Markus Brunnermeier and Dirk Nierpelt have shown—provided that the central bank commits credibly to act as a lender of last resort. This is something that the Fed has already made clear, through its actions, that it is committed to. As they explain in an important paper: "With a strong commitment, a transfer of funds from deposit to CBDC accounts would give rise to an automatic substitution of one type of bank funding (deposits) by another one (central bank funding)—the issuance of CBDC would simply render the central bank's implicit lender-of-last-resort guarantee explicit. By construction, a swap of CBDC for deposits thus would not reduce bank funding; it would only change the composition of bank funding."[11]

Thus fedcoin would not reduce credit, crowd out private-sector investment, or undermine financial stability.[12] The CBDC would be an asset with the same liquidity properties as bank deposits. Thus if the deposits of households are exchanged for the CBDC, then the allocation of resources should be the same, provided that the central bank provides loans to commercial banks equivalent to the deposit liabilities that are switched out, and household wealth and constraints remain unchanged.

Following a swap of fedcoins for bank deposits, the Fed would conduct monetary policy by adjusting the total quantity of fedcoins in order to set the target federal funds rate. All money would be created by the Fed through minting fedcoins, rather than by banks creating money. This system would differ from the current ample-reserves regime because most money in circulation would be a claim on the balance sheet of the Federal Reserve rather than on those of commercial banks. To create new loans, commercial banks could borrow fedcoins from the Fed at the federal funds rate, and lend them out. There would no economic difference in credit provision, but there would be a mechanical difference in the way the Fed set the short-term interest rate.

Much of the discussion about how a CBDC would affect banks has assumed a system that has both a CBDC and a traditional account-based banking system.[13] In such a hybrid system, the substitution between deposits and the CBDC is a matter of concern. Under a complete switch from deposit to a CBDC this coexistence problem is moot.

The idea of separating credit and money creation has a precedent. The so-called Chicago Plan, proposed by a number of University of Chicago economists after the Great Depression, proposed a complete separation of the monetary and credit functions of the banking system. The plan had two parts. First, deposits would be fully backed by government-issued money. Second, financing of new (bank) credit could occur only through borrowing of government-issued money, or from retained earnings. That is, credit could not be provided through the creation of money by commercial banks.

Perhaps ironically, this type of system would return the Fed's management of interest rates to the way it was done during the term of Paul Volcker as Fed chair in the late 1970s and early 1980s. When Volcker took over, the federal funds rate was managed by increasing or decreasing the amount of reserves in the banking system. To push official rates up, the Fed would create a shortage of reserves, and to lower them, it and would create a surplus. In 1979 Volcker instituted a change whereby the growth in the money supply (in reality, bank reserves) would be set, and the interest rate would adjust to equilibrate supply and demand. This was consistent with the conservative economist Milton Friedman's doctrine of *monetarism*, which held that inflation was very closely linked to growth of the money supply—captured in his aphorism "Inflation is always and everywhere a monetary phenomenon."[14]

There is one important way in which Fedcoin would expand the toolkit of central bankers. And that concerns what happens when they want to set interest rates really low. Since the early 1990s, many central banks in advanced economies—the Fed included—have set an explicit inflation target. That is, they try to adjust interest rates to keep inflation at a low (but not zero) level. In the United States, the target is 2 percent. In Australia it's between 2 and 3 percent. One of Raghuram Rajan's key accomplishments at the Reserve Bank of India was to boost its credibility by managing inflation. As he put it, "The best way for the central bank to generate growth in the long run is for it to keep inflation low and steady. . . . [I]n order to generate sustainable growth, we have to fight inflation first."[15]

Managing inflation sounds simple enough: if the rate is too high, then the central bank should raise interest rates. And that's exactly what Paul Volcker did, providing that a credible commitment to being tough on inflation could keep both inflation expectations and actual inflation low. But when inflation is *too* low, the central bank needs to cut interest rates in order to stimulate economic activity. The objective is to arrive at the "equilibrium real interest rate" or "neutral rate"—the inflation-adjusted interest rate that stimulates the economy enough to push prices up. The problem is that the neutral rate could be negative. In fact, it could be so far into the negative range that the *nominal* or non-inflation-adjusted interest rate required to match it would also need to be negative. A negative interest rate means that people *lose* money when they put it in the bank. If I save $100 for a year and the interest rate is 5 percent, I will have $105 at the end of the year. But if I save $100 and the interest rate is minus 2 percent, I will be left with $98. In this situation, people will respond by putting the money under the proverbial mattress—withdrawing it from the bank and keeping it in cash.

Because of the risks of holding cash, depositors may tolerate interest rates slightly below zero. This was the case in Europe in the early 2020s. But if a rate of minus 2 percent is required to manage the rate of inflation, there is little that central banks can do under the existing financial system. They can lower longer-term rates through asset purchases—a practice known as quantitative easing. But short-term rates can't go much below zero.

If rates need to be set below zero but cannot be, then inflation can actually turn negative—*deflation* can occur. But that reinforces the need for even lower interest rates, the absence of which further drives down prices, and so on. Such a deflationary spiral can be incredibly hard to get out of, as the experience of Japan from the 1990s onward has highlighted.

Fedcoin provides a way out of this bind. Because fedcoin would represent a direct claim on the Federal Reserve—and because it would be a digital coin—it could exist in fractional form. It would be straightforward for the Fed to declare that, over the course of a year, each fedcoin would become worth (say) 0.98 fedcoins. This would effectively implement a negative interest rate, one that would apply to all money in the system.

WHAT ABOUT THE BANKING SECTOR?

If banks no longer created credit, but were simply involved in interfacing with customers, nothing would really change with respect to daily activities. Commercial banks would still provide services to customers; they would be responsible for verifying customers' identity under KYC rules and matching it to account or digital wallet codes. And they would still perform the valuable function of making loans—determining credit quality and loan interest rates and approving lenders. Banks just wouldn't "create" money—that would be done purely by the Fed.

This change would have one negative effect on commercial banks, however, through the somewhat obscure concept of *seigniorage*. This takes its name from the middle French word *seigneur*, meaning feudal lord. Seigniorage refers to the amount of money the Fed makes from minting money.

It doesn't cost $20 to create a $20 bill: it costs way less. But when a $20 bill is created and issued to a bank for use by its customers, the bank pays $20 for it by electronically wiring the Fed $20. The Fed invests these funds in things like Treasury bonds, which earn interest. Seigniorage is the interest earned minus the cost of making the banknotes, shipping them out to banks, and replacing them when they wear out. Because interest rates vary, the amount of seigniorage fluctuates. But a reasonable estimate is that the US government earns about $25 billion a year in seigniorage.

From the point of view of the Fed, fedcoin would not affect seigniorage, except by eliminating the costs of printing paper (or polymer) money. But since commercial banks would no longer be creating credit, they would lose the seigniorage that they implicitly earn through money creation. The government could compensate for this loss, however, in any number of ways.

RETIRING CASH

Cast your mind back to the disastrous demonetarization ordered by Indian prime minister Narendra Modi. Even though parts of his motivation were sound—specifically, getting rid of ill-gotten gains parked in cash—the execution was deeply flawed. But there are lessons in that episode for how the United States can transition from paper money to Fedcoin.

First, an orderly transition to fedcoin would require plenty of time for physical cash to be exchanged. In India, there simply wasn't enough time allowed for people to exchange all the banknotes they needed to. In order for authorities to scrutinize the provenance of large amounts of cash, extra time and an orderly process would be required.

The second, and related, lesson concerns financial inclusion. Under fedcoin, everybody would need to be "banked"—that is, they would require access to a bank account and, at a minimum, a tap card. This would take time and require outreach programs. Undocumented residents of the United States might have legitimate concerns that establishing a bank account could trigger immigration enforcement or other legal problems. These fears would need to be assuaged, otherwise there would be people excluded from the financial system and unable to do business in cash.

In addition, there would be the question of how international institutional holders of US dollars would transfer their holdings to fedcoin. In most cases this would be simple enough. Central banks like the Bank of England would simply hold digital deposits with the Federal Reserve as they already do. But rogue governments like North Korea purportedly hold large amounts of US currency, some of it counterfeit. Would these holdings simply evaporate? Would some kind of deal be done? This would be a matter of high politics. But it would have little bearing on the ongoing functioning of a fedcoin-based financial system.

THE CASE FOR FEDCOIN

A US central bank digital currency on the model sketched here would have a number of major benefits. It would essentially eliminate the use of cash as a lubricant for trade in illegal drugs and arms, human trafficking, tax evasion, and other socially harmful activities. This benefit stems from the fact that fedcoin would be pseudo-anonymous, rather than completely anonymous as cash is. Within a strict legal framework, a government authority like the IRS could use the fedcoin ledger as evidence that a crime like tax evasion had been committed. Knowing that detection was not just a possibility but an almost certain outcome, individuals would be dramatically less likely to evade tax. The same goes for a range of other illicit activities that currently use cash as a medium of exchange. The very presence of a credible threat—that the IRS will catch you if you evade taxes—significantly reduces the need for enforcement. This is a piece of economic magic.

Matched against these advantages of fedcoin are concerns about privacy. It's tempting to reprise the quip by Scott McNealy, the CEO of Sun Microsystems, in 1999: "You have zero privacy anyway. Get over it."[16] But privacy is an important constitutional value in most liberal democracies.[17] Although the US Constitution may not contain an express right to privacy, the idea lives in the amendments that make up the Bill of Rights.[18]

Although, on balance, a fedcoin system would not represent a meaningful threat to privacy, it would be unwise to dismiss privacy concerns too quickly. It's true that technology companies have all kinds of personal details about us—including our browser search history—and may exploit it in annoying and even harmful ways. But those companies don't have the coercive power of the state. That power is one of the reasons for concern about government intrusion on our privacy.

The information at issue is simply what people spend money on. For the most part this is deeply uninteresting and innocuous. Of course, some people spend money on goods or services that they would be embarrassed to reveal to others. So the incremental concern is that government might know that somebody buys pornography or some other potentially embarrassing item. For all practical purposes, government has no interest in this kind of information, can already access it, and is in any case prevented from using it by existing laws in most democracies. The minor cost of a CBDC to individuals' privacy must be weighed against a meaningful reduction in tax evasion, illegal drug trafficking, and other socially destructive activities. Most people would agree that's a worthwhile trade to make.

Those benefits are what we might call the *offensive* rationale for fedcoin. But there is also a vital *defensive* rationale, which concerns the need to retain control over monetary policy by preempting competition from private digital currencies. It's true that even if a private digital currency gained widespread acceptance—as libra's creators envisioned—the US dollar would not cease to exist. If nothing else, it would continue to be used for federal tax payments, and the federal government would use it to make benefits payments to the public. The likely result of a private currency's gaining hold would be a monetary system similar to what existed in the nineteenth century under the gold standard.[19] Because fiat currencies were formally convertible into gold, it was the supply of and demand for gold that ultimately determined the value of goods and services. The dominant private digital currency would replace gold as this benchmark or *numéraire*.

And, just as in the nineteenth century, it would be the supply of and demand for that *numéraire* that would effectively determine monetary policy. As the former Fed chair Ben Bernanke put it, in this setting "monetary policies aimed at stabilizing prices or employment would no longer be feasible, since central banks would have no control over the supply of money." He went on to say that because the public expects the government to attempt to stabilize the economy, this arrangement would be politically unsustainable. The problem would be, at that point, how to unwind the arrangement. It would, at a minimum, require the significant assistance of the controller of the private currency, who would be in a position to extract enormous rents for providing that assistance.[20]

Unfortunately, there is no easy regulatory solution to this problem. For instance, a regulation stipulating that a stable coin must be backed 100 percent by Treasury bills might appear to create a one-to-one relationship between Treasuries and the private currency, but it does not. If the stable coin becomes the predominant medium of exchange, then the government *still* loses control of the money supply. To maintain monetary sovereignty, the government would need a kind of corollary regulation that if government issued more Treasury bills, then the stable coin would have to increase its supply. But that decision would be under the control of the stable coin controller.

Fedcoin could preempt the development of a private digital currency by removing any legitimate rationale for it. Fedcoin would allow developers all the functionality needed for Web3. It would be premised on financial inclusion within the United States, would provide a model for other nations' CBDCs, and would provide the backbone for cheaper and more efficient international money transfers. And it would preserve the US dollar—in digital form—as the global reserve currency.

There are many other possible models of CBDCs. A particularly pluralistic one is known as a regulated liability network (RLN). Under an RLN a CBDC coexists with stable coins, tokenized commercial bank money, and e-money in the wallets of e-money customers. Payments on the RLN happen not through bearer instruments but through the transfer of liabilities between institutions. In an RLN, the key function of a CBDC is to support the transfer of tokenized private liabilities.[21] An RLN has the virtue of minimally altering the existing monetary system. But, as this chapter has emphasized, having a significant effect on the existing system is part of the rationale for fedcoin. So in that sense fedcoin and an RLN are at opposite ends of the range of CBDC options.

6

THE EXORBITANT
PRIVILEGE

IF THE US DEPARTMENT of the Treasury ever hired a publicist to bolster its image, its slogan might be a play on Dunkin' Donuts' "America runs on Dunkin.'" It's not just America but the entire world that almost literally runs on US dollars.

Roughly 60 percent of the world's nearly $13 trillion in current government and central-bank currency reserves are denominated in dollars. The euro is in a distant second place with about 20 percent of reserves. The Japanese yen is third with just 5 percent. About half of all cross-border bank loans are in dollars, compared to just one-third for the euro.[1]

Janet Yellen's American University speech summarizes the greenback's global dominance: "The dollar . . . is by far the most traded currency, accounting for nearly 90% of one leg in foreign exchange transactions and over half of trading invoices. US dollar-denominated assets account for about half of cross-border bank claims and more than 40% of outstanding international debt securities. And with the dollar's strong trade and financial linkages—as well as strong US macroeconomic and monetary credibility—central banks have chosen to hold nearly 60% of their foreign exchange reserves in dollars."[2]

This dominance arose in the aftermath of World War II. The postwar financial order was essentially crafted by the United States and the other Allied powers at a conference in Bretton Woods, New Hampshire, in 1944. Mindful of the fact that the gold standard had fallen apart during the Great Depression, the Allies were keen to find an effective but more flexible replacement. The Bretton Woods agreement involved the US dollar's being pegged to gold and other currencies being pegged to the US dollar. That put the United States in an enviable position—so much so that in the early 1960s the French finance minister, Valéry Giscard d'Estaing, suggested that the global-reserve currency status gave the United States an "exorbitant privilege."[3]

There are good reasons for the international system as a whole to have one dominant currency, or what is sometimes referred to as a *hegemon*. In the words of Charles Kindleberger, an MIT economist and a famous scholar of international financial crises, it is useful and important to have a currency that will provide "liquidity when the monetary system is frozen in panic."[4] The US dollar, for a variety of reasons, has played that role since the end of World War II.

Not surprisingly, there are also benefits for the hegemon. Those benefits break down into four categories.[5] First, the United States earns some (extra) seigniorage because other countries hold dollars in what amounts to interest-free loans to the United States. That's arguably not very much—perhaps about $20 billion a year—but it's still worth having.[6] Second, it stabilizes the terms of trade for the United States. Third, it gives the United States additional geopolitical power, including the ability to enforce sanctions against other countries and specifically, those countries' financial institutions. Sanctions against Iran were a good example of this power, as were the more recent sanctions against Russia. Fourth—and this is perhaps the biggest benefit of all—the

United States can have a lot of debt outstanding because—by the definition of a global reserve currency—people buy a lot of US government debt. This means that the United States is able to finance long-run budget deficits at a lower cost. Put differently, it can get away with having a higher ratio of net debt to GDP for a given interest rate than other countries can.[7]

The Bretton Woods system collapsed in the early 1970s when President Nixon pulled the United States off the gold standard. Yet even without centralized enforcement of its use as the global reserve currency, the dollar has retained this status, in part simply because of the benefits to everyone of having one undisputed global reserve currency. In effect this is a coordination game. European countries would prefer it to be the euro, and Japan would prefer it to be the yen, but the lack of an agreed reserve currency would be worse. As Ben Bernanke put it, "the most important reason" for the dollar's continued preeminence "is certainly inertia."[8]

And in that inertia lies danger. Just as network externalities influence people's use of a digital payment system or a particular ride-sharing platform, they also influence the adoption of a global reserve currency.[9] The US dollar is seen as a safe and stable currency in part because so many countries hold foreign currency reserves in it, which in turn makes it an attractive currency in which to hold reserves. The foreign exchange market involving the US dollar is efficient because it is highly liquid, and liquidity creates efficiency. But by the same self-reinforcing logic, if another nation's currency became the global reserve currency, *it* would be hard to dislodge. In other words, inertia favors the incumbent.[10] That's good news if you're the incumbent, but bad news if you're not.

The legal scholar Bruce Akerman has spoken of "constitutional moments" in which great change can occur to constitutional arrangements in a short period.[11] Similarly, the evolutionary biologists Niles Eldredge and Stephen Jay Gould spoke of "punctuated equilibria," periods during which evolution of a species can proceed in leaps rather than gradually.[12] The move to CBDCs is precisely the kind of "economic moment" that could allow another country's currency to displace the US dollar as the global reserve currency.

The stable political system in the United States, its sound legal and financial institutions, and the widespread use of English as the language of international commerce all reinforce the US dollar's status. But other countries have many of the same attributes, and in recent years some of them have been called into question in the United States. Absent a major event—say, the United States defaulting on its foreign debt—it is unlikely that the dollar would suddenly lose favor. But if China or the European Union adopted a well-crafted CBDC, that could be the type of economic moment that could lead to the dethroning of the dollar. China under President Xi Jinping has made no secret of its global ambitions, its refusal to bow to American supremacy in any realm, and its apparently sincere belief that it has an economic system superior to those of the United States and other Western liberal democracies.

I am not necessarily suggesting that the United States (or Europe for that matter) has a right to special status in the global financial system. I simply take it as self-evident that the United States seeks to protect the special status that it enjoys, and I suggest that global CBDC dominance is a necessary condition for preserving this status.

The CBDC race isn't just about exorbitant privilege or economic prestige, although these have measurable benefits. It's about whose currency is going to be the central pillar in an age of Web3-enabled commerce. And although the vast majority of international financial contracts are written in dollars today, the question is whether the smart contracts of tomorrow will be written in fedcoins or e-CNY (the digital yuan).

Anyone who doubts China's intentions should look no further than the battle over 5G telecommunications networks. China is a leading manufacturer of equipment for these networks, but a number of countries have banned the use of Chinese 5G equipment on national security grounds. In 2018 Australia banned equipment from the Chinese companies Huawei and ZTE, stating that companies "likely to be subject to extrajudicial directions from a foreign government" posed unacceptable security risks.[13] This move was seen as a serious affront to China, and the Chinese government has made a number of demands of the Australian government in response.[14]

We've already seen that financial sanctions against countries like Iran and Russia can significantly affect the functioning, and potentially the political stability, of those countries. In a world of smart contracts, digital money has a greater role than traditional money, and the country (or other entity) whose digital currency becomes the global reserve currency will wield even more power than the United States does today.

A GLOBAL RESERVE CURRENCY IN THE DIGITAL AGE
Central Bank Digital Currencies and Smart Contracts

Chapter 4 showed how smart contracts—underpinned by a private cryptocurrency like bitcoin or, more likely, by a CBDC like fedcoin or the e-CNY—can mitigate hold-up problems. That is, they can allow parties to ensure that they have appropriate incentives to invest in their trading relationship—in particular, to make what are known as "relationship-specific investments." This capability has the potential not only to increase economic efficiency but also to change the nature of asset ownership and the boundaries of the firm.

Chapter 5 discussed how tokenized CBDCs would allow for some seemingly mundane but very valuable uses of smart money and smart contracts. By allowing conditionality to be built into the exchange of tokens, it is feasible to ensure that the actual exchange of a CBDC occurs only when certain conditions are satisfied. This is important in the simultaneous exchange of currencies (PvP exchanges) and also very useful in securities trading. These features are applicable to *all* spot contracting—that is, any situation where payment and the delivery of goods or services happen almost simultaneously. Although a private cryptocurrency could form the basis for such exchanges, a central bank digital currency could perform the same role.

A CBDC could also facilitate the enforcement of so-called *liquidated damages* (sometimes more accurately referred to as *stipulated damages*). These are clauses that require one party to a contract to pay another party a large financial sum if they default on their contractual obligations. Many common-law courts (in jurisdictions like the United States and United Kingdom) refuse to enforce liquidated damages clauses that are in excess of the economic damages incurred by nonperformance of the contract. This is something of a puzzle for economists since it is exactly such clauses that best encourage compliance. Smart contracts offer a potential way to enforce them.[15]

If new smart contracting opportunities materialize, then the country whose digital currency is the standard medium of exchange will suddenly see increased demand. And because smart contracts have the potential to supplant some economic activity that currently takes place within firms, they would represent a new use of that currency. In other words, the prize for the issuer of the world's reserve currency is likely to get much bigger in the era of digital currencies. The exorbitant privilege may become more exorbitant. This prospect is likely to generate more intense competition between countries for that prize.

The dominant issuer of digital currency emerging from smart contracts will also have jurisdiction over the contracts. This might at first seem puzzling. Smart contracts are self-executing code that don't require—and whose signatories don't typically want—the involvement of third parties like courts. But as smart contracts become increasingly used by sophisticated parties, it is likely that a form of "hybrid smart contracts" will arise: contracts that specify circumstances under which the code is self-executing and self-enforcing, and other circumstances, such as disputes between the parties, under which there is recourse to courts or commercial arbitration. Such arrangements would take advantage of the benefits of smart contracts without the limitation of not being able to renegotiate if unforeseen circumstances arise, or if a mistake is made in the code. Contracts that are renegotiation-proof are powerful but, by their nature, inflexible.

If hybrid smart contracts do become popular, it would be natural (though perhaps not essential) for disputes to be adjudicated by the courts of the country that issues the digital currency used in the contract. Having jurisdiction over important commercial arrangements can bring substantial economic benefits. This is apparent for the State of Delaware for contracts within the United States and for the State of New York in international commercial arrangements. The benefits to contracting parties of jurisdiction by an entity with an established body of law has been well documented.[16]

Central Bank Digital Currencies and Sanctions

Smart contracts powered by CBDCs will not only provide an expanded contracting reach but also enable broader enforcement of sanctions against countries that violate the norms of the international community.

As discussed earlier, the international community was able to enforce sanctions against Iran and Russia in recent years through a variety of measures. In late June, 2022 Treasury Secretary Janet Yellen detailed measures to constrain Russia's military capacities in its war against Ukraine, part of a package of sanctions enacted by the United States and other nations. "We once again reaffirm our commitment to working alongside our partners and allies to impose additional severe sanctions in response to Russia's war against Ukraine. Broad multilateral commitments and actions by G7 members this week further cut off the Russian Federation's access to technology that is critical to their military. Targeting Russia's defense industry will degrade Putin's capabilities and further impede his war against Ukraine, which has already been plagued by poor morale, broken supply chains, and logistical failures."[17]

How did these sanctions this work, exactly? And what role did money play? The measures to which Yellen referred were fairly direct bans on US corporations and citizens doing business with certain Russian corporations. In addition, they restricted the movement of a number of Russian individuals (e.g., by canceling visas) and banned gold imports from Russia into the United States.

These actions followed from Executive Orders 14024 and 14065, issued by President Joe Biden. They were targeted largely at individuals and organizations playing a critical role in Russia's defense industry—especially the state-owned corporation Rostec. The US Treasury described Rostec as "the cornerstone of Russia's defense, industrial, technology, and manufacturing sectors."[18]

These are important moves, and they are part of a package of sanctions measures enacted by the United States and its allies. But from the moment the sanctions against Russia were announced, concerns were raised about China's willingness to cooperate. There was a precedent: when sanctions were imposed against Iran, Turkish companies and Turkish nationals were at the center of a massive and damaging scheme to circumvent them. Between 2012 and 2013 Iran managed to generate $12 billion from gold sales that were supposedly prohibited by sanctions, using the funds to further its nuclear program.[19] To their credit, prosecutors in Turkey exposed the scheme and held a number of individuals to account. These prosecutors also documented how entities in Dubai and China participated in money-laundering schemes involving Iranian oil and gas sales.[20]

US and international sanctions at the time sought to keep Iranian foreign currency reserves in escrow accounts held overseas. In theory, the Iranian regime could use those accounts only in local currency to buy local products. But Turkish front companies issued invoices for fictitious transactions for goods permitted under the sanctions, like food and medicines. This tactic, known as overinvoicing, has been used for decades in money-laundering and tax-evasion schemes around the world. One entity engages in trade with another for legitimate goods, but it pays way too much for them. The excess funds can be "washed" to look as though they came from trade in legitimate goods. An article in the May 2013 issue of *Foreign Policy* documents an "invoice detailing a luxury yacht company selling nearly 5.2 tons of brown sugar to Iran's Bank Pasargad, with delivery to Dubai, using Turkey's state-owned Halkbank at the whopping price of 1,170 Turkish lira per kilo—the equivalent of approximately $240 per pound."[21]

Through transactions like this, Iranian banks managed to evade the sanctions and accumulate large amounts of hard currency from Halkbank. Instead of being held in escrow at Halkbank, Iranian funds from oil and gas sales to Turkey were transferred as approved transactions on legitimate goods. The bank's transaction receipts even stipulated that the "goods and services are not related to EUR Reg 423/2007 and 428/2009"— the European Union regulations relating to sanctions against Iran.[22]

Once sanctions have been violated, the problem only gets worse. In this case, because some Iranian banks, like Karafarin, Pasargad, Parsian, and Saman, were not cut off from the SWIFT electronic messaging system used for funds transfers, it was easy enough for funds to be converted into US dollars and euros and then transferred to those banks via SWIFT. At that point the money was completely outside the sanctions regime.

Stopping this sort of activity is hard. To prevent an overinvoicing scheme requires detailed knowledge of "fair" prices for food and medicine and close scrutiny of all trades. This is almost impossible. Moreover, cutting off a country from trade in all goods would create a humanitarian disaster and thereby undercut public support for the sanctions in the countries imposing them. It's hard to claim moral authority in world affairs if you deny innocent citizens access to food and medicines.

The stories exposing sanction busting show how difficult it is to catch the people involved. Reza Zarrab, a Turkish-Iranian dual citizen at the heart of the operation to help Iran evade sanctions, was brought to account only because of an ill-advised family vacation at Disney World in 2017. As the story in *The Atlantic* recounted, "With the 2015 nuclear deal in effect, he may have believed that the sanctions laws he violated before the deal were no longer in force. Some suggest that Zarrab was trying to flee Iranian justice, particularly as the regime came to grasp just how much he skimmed off the top. Either way, when he arrived in Florida, US authorities arrested him for engaging in conspiracies to violate sanctions, commit bank fraud, and launder money."[23] Stories like this, combined with what we know about digital money and smart contracts, raise the question of whether CBDCs might make it harder to enforce sanctions against rogue nations—and the still harder question of whether a Chinese CBDC that challenged the US dollar for supremacy as the global reserve currency would prevent US-led sanctions from having much bite at all.

Never have there been more tools and information available to those enforcing economic sanctions. And, arguably, never in recent history has there been greater consensus and cohesion in the international community about enforcing these sanctions. The US Treasury outlines six planks to the current sanctions against Russia.

1. Full blocking sanctions on Russia's largest financial institution, Sberbank, and Russia's largest private bank, Alfa Bank.
2. Prohibiting new investment in the Russian Federation.
3. Full blocking sanctions on major Russian state-owned enterprises.
4. Full blocking sanctions on Russian elites and their family members.
5. A prohibition on Russia's making debt payments with funds subject to US jurisdiction
6. A commitment to supporting sectors essential to humanitarian activities.[24]

The US Treasury's authority to prevent US corporations and individuals from doing business with a sanctioned country like Russia is an extremely powerful part of the sanctions program. An equilibrium arises in which US corporations and individuals are either prohibited from doing business with entities in the sanctioned country or simply unwilling to do so. Even if a Chinese CBDC became the global reserve currency, it would be unlikely to undermine this power available to the US government, which emanates from the size of the US economy and the importance of the United States as a home jurisdiction for companies and citizens.

But a number of the other provisions of the sanctions regime are more tenuous. If the SWIFT messaging service—based in Belgium and subject to Belgian (and hence European) law—were effectively replaced by transfers through wholesale central bank digital currencies, many elements of sanctions enforcement would change. If the Turkish entities assisting Iran to evade sanctions had been able to make transfers through a CBDC, they wouldn't have needed to go through the charade of overinvoicing for sugar. How would such a transfer be prohibited in the world of an e-ruble?

To avoid this contingency, one approach would be to focus on the network of central banks that verifies transactions. This would require nodes to see various e-ruble transactions as invalid. Whether this approach is workable would depend on the details of the consensus protocol. It would also depend on the governance structure of the blockchain itself. Would it be "owned" by the constituent central banks, and would they be able to vote out the central banks of other countries—and with them, the commercial banks in those countries?

Since wholesale CBDCs are still in the development phase, none of these details are known at this point. But they are extremely important. It is clear that excluding a country's banks from financial transactions would be more complicated than simply instructing SWIFT to cut off certain Russian banks.

A further complication could arise if central banks were willing to make bilateral exchanges between commercial banks in their respective countries. Suppose, for instance, that China refused to agree to sanctions on Russia and allowed China's Central Bank, the People's Bank of China (PBOC), to make digital transfers between commercial banks in China and their counterparts in Russia. The only obvious remedy available to the international community would be to cut off China from CBDC settlements—that is, to suspend the whole of China from the international financial system. This would be a draconian move. Would the United States have been willing to ban all Chinese companies from doing business in the US, and vice versa, if China had simply refused to comply with sanctions on Russia in 2022? The answer to that question is almost surely not.

The development of interbank networks that settle CBDC transactions will be an important matter of international financial diplomacy. The nature of a network like SWIFT entails substantial political advantages for Western liberal democracies. But SWIFT will be replaced by some form of blockchain that settles digital currency transactions. Will that be a single blockchain? How will it be governed? What will the choice of governing law mean for the organization behind it? These are all important and challenging questions. But there is one more, which may prove the most challenging of all. Will China be willing to be part of a multilateral organization on terms that give the West the ability to enforce sanctions against rogue nations?

BEATING CHINA IN THE CBDC RACE
The Chinese CBDC Project

China has a significant head start in the race to implement the first fully functional central bank digital currency. Two Chinese companies have paved the way with widely used private digital payments systems—Alipay (owned by Ant Financial/Alibaba) and WeChat Pay (owned by Tencent). Although these systems are mobile money (digital wallets) rather than digital money, their market share has demonstrated how powerful network externalities can be. Both companies have more than one billion users, and Alipay has performed more than half a million transactions per second.

The PBOC began moving to establish a digital currency, the e-CNY, in 2014, by convening a task force to study issuance, technological requirements, and comparable international experiences. In 2016 the PBOC established a Digital Currency Institute that outlined a prototype of the Chinese CBDC. In late 2017 the bank began partnering with commercial institutions to develop and test the digital currency, known as the e-CNY.

Unlike Alipay and WeChat Pay, the e-CNY is legal tender and must be accepted by every commercial entity in China. The e-CNY and the paper yuan are exchangeable at a one-to-one rate. At ATMs that convert the e-CNY into cash, users simply scan a QR code, using the digital yuan wallet.[25] The digital currency can be purchased through China's six big state-owned banks, as well as through Tencent and Ant Financial/Alibaba.

The e-CNY network is based on a model that has been described as "one coin, two databases, three centers." The "one coin" is simply the single government-issued coin or token. The "two databases" are the PBOC's centralized ledger and the ledgers that are maintained by the lower-tier banks in the network. The "three centers" are data centers that supposedly hold a database of the true identities of digital wallet holders, track transactions, analyze financial risks, and monitor illicit transactions.[26]

The PBOC has stated clearly that the "e-CNY is mainly a substitute for cash in circulation (Mo), and will coexist with physical RMB [yuan/renminbi]. . . . As long as there is demand for the physical RMB, the PBOC will neither stop supplying it, nor replace it via administrative order." This, of course, raises the question of for how long and under what conditions demand for the physical RMB will persist, although the PBOC has been explicit about the logistical and cultural challenges in moving exclusively to a digital currency.[27]

The e-CNY was first introduced in Beijing, Shenzhen, Shanghai, Suzhou, Xiong'an, Chengdu, Hainan, Changsha, Xi'an, Qingdao, and Dalian. In March 2022 the PBOC announced it would expand the trial to include Chongqing, Tianjin, Hangzhou, and Guangzhou. The Chinese government used financial incentives to spur adoption among consumers. This strategy has been used by Silicon Valley firms in markets with network externalities. For instance, to build up its network in its early days, PayPal waived transaction fees and offered a five-dollar signup bonus. As the business journalist Adam Cohen observes, "Handing out free money was costly, but fairly effective: by the end of 1999, PayPal had signed up twelve thousand registered users."[28] The PBOC has signaled a focus on continued further adoption: "Policies must be designed to stimulate creativity and enthusiasm among the banks, technology firms and the local government in the development, promotion and proliferation of the digital yuan."[29] And the PBOC's Digital Currency Research Institute (DCRI) has recently hired hundreds of data and infrastructure engineers.

Perhaps an even stronger indication of the PBOC's intentions is its plans to introduce the e-CNY in the global financial center of Hong Kong. Eddie Yue Wai-man, head of the Hong Kong Monetary Authority (effectively Hong Kong's central bank) said in February 2022 that "the pilot testing of e-CNY will be an important move for Hong Kong to strengthen its role as an international offshore yuan trading centre."[30] These extensive plans look a lot more like the rollout of a fully fledged CBDC than an experiment.

The most important question at this point is where this initiative will end. It is possible that the Chinese government is simply uncomfortable with the level of control that Alibaba and Tencent have over the payments system and wants to effectively take over the market share of those businesses without resorting to a dramatic move like nationalizing them. If that is the case, the e-CNY would not represent a competitor to a US CBDC, and the defensive rationale for establishing fedcoin—and doing so relatively quickly—would be somewhat weakened. Other countries that might soon issue CBDCs, such as Sweden, Singapore, or South Korea, would be unlikely to compete effectively with a nondigital US dollar for the status of global reserve currency. China is a different category in terms of both economic scale and political ambition.

A second, and more likely, possibility is that the Chinese government is intent on moving to a fully fledged retail CBDC. The government has said that the e-CNY is designed to "create a new form of RMB that meets the public's demand for cash in the era of the digital economy. Supported by a retail payment infrastructure that is reliable, efficient, adaptive and open, the e-CNY system will bolster China's digital economy, enhance financial inclusion, and make the monetary and payment systems more efficient."[31]

The decline of cash has meant that the central bank has essentially lost market share to private providers. Hence the PBOC's announced intention to "diversify the forms of cash provided to the public by the central bank, satisfy the public's demand for digital cash and support financial inclusion."[32] It is also clear that the PBOC views the e-CNY as a vehicle for cross-border payments and a way "to promote RMB internationalization." Moreover, it shows a clear understanding of the roles of scale and network externalities in determining the global reserve currency, observing that "the internationalization of a currency is a natural result of market selection. The international status of a country's currency depends on its economic fundamentals and the depth, efficiency and openness of its financial markets. Therefore, though technically ready for cross-border use, e-CNY is still designed mainly for domestic retail payments at present. Looking ahead, the PBOC will actively respond to initiatives of the G20 and other international organizations on improving cross-border payments, and explore the applicability of CBDC in cross-border scenarios."[33]

The steady rollout of the e-CNY has been aided by co-opting Alibaba and Tencent. The Chinese government has put these companies in a tricky position. Their services are extremely popular with the public, and banning them overnight would be disruptive. Alipay and WeChat Pay fill a significant gap in the domestic payments system, and their disappearance would be a major step backward. The PBOC has positioned the e-CNY not as a competitor to Alipay and WeChat Pay but a complementary part of the payments ecosystem. This approach has made it natural for the PBOC to seek the cooperation of Alibaba and Tencent in the rollout of the e-CNY and borderline impossible for those companies to withhold that cooperation.

There is, of course, a backstory to all of this. Ant Financial—the parent company of Alipay, which was spun out of Alibaba years ago—was due to go public in 2021. This promised to be the largest-grossing initial public offering (IPO) in history, tipped to raise $34 billion. However, this plan was scuttled after Alibaba's founder and chair, Jack Ma, criticized Chinese financial regulators in a speech in October 2020. Ma said that they focused far too much on minimizing risk and failed to recognize that "there is no innovation in this world without risk." He likened Chinese commercial banks to pawnshops in their excessive collateral requirements for lending. Perhaps Ma thought that his status and wealth would enable him to deliver these (accurate) criticisms without consequences. But state-owned media quickly picked up on the speech and were highly critical of it. Not long afterward, financial regulators summoned Ma and Ant Financial executives. The next day the Shanghai Stock Exchange called off the IPO. As the *New York Times* reported, the government sent a clear message: "No private business gets to swagger unless the government is on board with it."[34]

Chinese authorities didn't stop there. In 2021 they hit the Alibaba Group with a record-breaking antitrust penalty of 18.2 billion yuan

(US\$2.8 billion). The State Administration for Market Regulation accused Alibaba of abusing market power by punishing merchants if they didn't sell exclusively through the company.[35]

And while there has been some suggestion that the Ant Financial IPO may be revived in the future, the government has made it clear that private financial firms—even giant ones with hugely popular and widely used products—operate at the pleasure of Chinese authorities. In this context, the participation of Alipay and WeChat Pay in the e-CNY rollout is understandable: they have no alternative.

The e-CNY has been positioned as being more protective of privacy than Alipay and WeChat Pay. The PBOC describes the principle as "anonymity for small value and traceable for high value." At the same time, it asserts that "it is necessary to guard against the misuse of e-CNY in illegal and criminal activities, such as tele-fraud, Internet gambling, money laundering, and tax evasion." The PBOC claims that less transaction information is collected during an e-CNY transaction than by private digital payments providers. It also claims to maintain an internal firewall for information associated with e-CNY transactions and states that the PBOC "strictly implements information security and privacy protocols, such as designating special personnel to manage information, separating e-CNY from other businesses, applying a tiered authorization system, putting in place checks and balances, and conducting internal audits."[36] The credibility of these commitments depends, of course, on one's view of the attitudes and responsibilities of the government.

Claiming that the e-CNY offers greater anonymity than private providers is an interesting point of product differentiation. Certainly, if the public values anonymity for small transactions and believes that the e-CNY will be as anonymous as the physical yuan while offering all the other advantages of digital money, its adoption will proceed more rapidly.

It is not hard to imagine a scenario in which, over a few years, the PBOC orchestrates a transition to a retail e-CNY that displaces private providers. After rolling out the e-CNY in most of China's major cities, the PBOC could move to increase its attractiveness. One natural way to do this would be to pay interest on balances in e-CNY wallets. This move entails a number of risks. It would make the CBDC more attractive than deposits in banks and so could damage the banking sector.[37] But it would certainly create an incentive for people to hold the digital fiat currency rather than the physical RMB. By instituting some of the proposed features of fedcoin discussed in chapter 5, it would be possible to preserve the stability of the banking sector. Alternatively, the PBOC might decide that the "full retail" model, in which the public all have individual accounts with the PBOC and the banking sector is largely cut out of the picture, was more attractive. Certainly, if it decided to go in this direction, the value proposition of private digital payments companies would be unclear, as would the question of what, if any, political or legal recourse they would have.

The Chinese government has additional tools at its disposal to squeeze out private providers like Alibaba and Tencent. First, the purportedly greater anonymity of the e-CNY could be used to highlight its advantages in a marketing campaign targeted at consumers. Second, linking the retail e-CNY to a wholesale digital currency for cross-border transactions could give it a powerful advantage over commercial payments systems. If it were faster, easier, and cheaper to make international transfers directly from an e-CNY wallet than by using a private provider, then customers would be unlikely to go through the two-step process of transferring funds from a private-provider wallet to an e-CNY wallet for international payments.

Competing with the e-CNY

Any analysis of how fedcoin—or the existing physical US dollar—would compete with the e-CNY has to start with the functionality of these different currencies. China might turn the e-CNY into a full-fledged retail currency while the United States stuck with the physical dollar. That is, China would continue its current rollout of the e-CNY, squeeze out Alipay and WeChat Pay, and accommodate their domestic banks as planned, while the US made no serious or effective move toward a CBDC. Meanwhile China would probably overtake the United States as the world's largest economy in terms of total output.

This would give China an efficiency advantage in its payments system, and it would improve the government's ability to crack down on tax evasion and illicit activities. It would also put the e-CNY in prime position to be at the center of a wholesale CBDC settlement regime along the lines of an expanded mBridge. The PBOC is already a key player in that project. And without even a wholesale CBDC, the United States would be unable to participate or organize a competing network. This would leave China with the most high-tech, highly functional modern domestic currency—a currency that would also be a convenient medium with which to settle international foreign exchange transactions. In short, it would be an economic moment that could help make the e-CNY the world's global reserve currency. That would have considerable negative consequences for the United States and arguably the world.

A different scenario might involve China adopting the full retail model, as just described, while the United States adopted a wholesale CBDC. This move might be enough to forestall the rise of the e-CNY as the global reserve currency while leaving the United States with a less modern, less functional domestic currency. This option would still be preferable to simply ceding currency leadership.

A third scenario would involve the US adopting fedcoin, as proposed in chapter 5, and the PBOC successfully rolling out the e-CNY ahead of fedcoin's eventual establishment. This is, in my view, the most likely outcome. It is also the best outcome for the United States. It would give the United States a strong chance of retaining its status as the global reserve currency. Domestically it would increase financial inclusion, improve transactional efficiency, and cut down on a range of illicit activities. It would also effectively foreclose the possibility of a private digital currency, preventing all the associated ill effects and loss of policy sovereignty.

The development of fedcoin will not be easy or cheap. Quite apart from the necessary research and development, it will entail transition costs and long-term running costs. Of course, a system based on physical cash has its own costs, spread all through the economy, and many of these would be eliminated after a complete transition to a digital currency.

The ongoing cost of a CBDC—in the United States and in other jurisdictions—is an interesting question. It will necessarily involve blockchain technology, and we know that operating decentralized ledger technology is expensive; but unlike Bitcoin, fedcoin would run on a centralized ledger. And there are other, less computationally expensive consensus protocols than the proof-of-work protocol used by Bitcoin. The cost of running the Fedcoin network could be small relative to the private equivalent.

7

CHEAP MONEY, ASSET
BUBBLES, AND
GOVERNMENT FINANCES

FOR THE ROUGHLY HALF a century that began with the election of John F. Kennedy as president and ended with the financial crisis of 2008, official interest rates in the United States averaged more than 6 percent.[1] As figure 4 shows, rates fluctuated considerably. Recessions (shaded gray) were often precipitated by a rise in official rates to cool down an overheated economy.

In setting interest rates, the Fed—like any central bank in an advanced economy—takes account of many factors, including economic (GDP) growth, unemployment, consumer sentiment, and business confidence. But for the last several decades at least, it has followed a fairly-basic general model. That model has two inputs.

The first is the *real interest rate*—that is, the nominal interest rate set by the Fed, adjusted for what the public expects inflation to be. The real interest rate is critical because it represents the opportunity cost of spending money this year

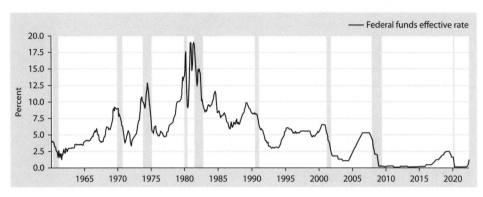

Figure 4. US official interest rates (federal funds effective rate), 1960–2022. Shaded areas indicate US recessions. *Source*: Board of Governors of the Federal Reserve System, https://fred.stlouisfed.org/series/USREC.

rather than next year. In other words, it's what people give up in the future to spend money now. It's the critical input into the spending and investment decisions of households and businesses.

The second input into the Fed's model of interest rates is the *output gap*. This is the difference between actual economic output and potential economic output—the amount that the economy could sustainably produce when all resources are put to work. When actual economic output is below potential, the economy is said to be running too cold. When actual output is above potential output, the economy is running too hot. When the economy runs too hot, there is a risk of inflation getting out of control. Businesses will do what they can to keep up. They might put off important maintenance, run extra shifts in production plants, and pay workers premiums to workers. But eventually these measures lead to problems, especially and including inflation.

The Fed's task is to set the nominal interest rate—that's what they control—to bring the real interest rate to a level that minimizes the output gap. This isn't an easy task. For one thing, the relationship between real interest rates and output is uncertain. History offers some guidance, but the world is constantly changing. A second issue is that although the Fed controls nominal interest rates, what they care about is real interest rates. The difference between those two rates is what the public *thinks* inflation is going to be. Those "inflation expectations," which depend on long-term beliefs about the economic and economic policy, are hard to pin down. A third issue is what potential output is. This is determined by long-term economic fundamentals and technological factors. In practice, the Fed attempts to determine the so-called neutral real interest rate, decides how it wants to influence the public's inflation expectations through its inflation target, and sets nominal interest rates accordingly.

There's a fair bit of guesswork in all of this. The former treasury secretary Larry Summers compared monetary to policy to "taking a shower in an old hotel where there's a twenty- or thirty-second lag between when you turn the faucet and when the temperature of the water changes. And it's very difficult in that situation to avoid either scalding yourself or freezing yourself. Because you turn it and you turn it and you turn it, and you don't feel anything, and then you try and turn it again and then, all of a sudden, the water has overadjusted."[2]

Overadjustments aside, the nominal interest rate is the real rate plus an adjustment for inflation. That adjustment for inflation should be equal to the inflation target of the central bank. Increasingly, since the early 1990s, central banks around the world have held themselves to an explicit inflation target. This is generally a low, stable figure: in the United States it's 2 percent, and in some other countries it's between 2 percent and 3 percent.

More to the point, it is the *real* interest rate that determines how much interest rates drive economic activity This rate can't be observed—we can't measure it directly the way we can rainfall, or even GDP. But it can be estimated. And the overwhelming consensus among economists is that the "equilibrium real rate of interest"— the real rate that is neither contractionary nor expansionary for the economy—has fallen considerably in recent decades.

SECULAR STAGNATION

In a speech at the International Monetary Fund, Larry Summers described this situation as one of "secular stagnation." This term was first used by another distinguished Harvard economist, Alvin Hansen, in the 1930s. According to Summers, what we were witnessing in the 2000s was a low-growth, low-inflation, low-interest-rate economy. When we did see strong economic growth, it had typically been caused by reckless financial bubbles like the US housing bubble between 2003 and 2007.

Secular stagnation arises when advanced economies like that of the United States suffer from an imbalance between savings and investment. There is an increase in the supply of investment capital and a reduction in the demand.

The demand for money basically stems from investment. The industrial economy was built with huge sums of money for large factories, machines, and equipment. This was the economy dominated by companies like J. D. Rockefeller's Standard Oil, by the telecommunications giant AT&T, and by steelmakers like Bethlehem and US Steel. By contrast, in the digital era, companies like Apple, Amazon, Microsoft, Google, and Facebook were created with comparatively small amounts of financial capital. Companies like this are based on an idea, not a mechanical or industrial process. In the digital era, great companies can be created with less financial capital—less money—than before.

The supply of money stems from savings, and those savings have increased. As people in advanced economies are living longer, they are saving more, because they expect to spend more years in retirement. Sometimes they save for themselves, and sometimes government effectively saves on their behalf through pension schemes. Another factor that has led to increased savings is an increase in the concentration of wealth since the 1980s. Because people with a billion dollars don't need to spend as much of their money as people living paycheck to paycheck, they save more.

This combination of new technologies, changing demographics, and an increase in the concentration of wealth have changed the balance of supply and demand in the market for money. And supply and demand determine the real price of loans. This is the *natural rate of interest*—the rate at which the supply of money and the demand for money are matched.

This reduction in the real rate of interest fundamentally affects how central banks behave. Most importantly, it has led them to set interest rates lower. In fact, because central banks can't easily set interest rates below zero, it has led them to adopt a range of other tools that have made money cheaper. With a steady stream of cheap money comes the risk of asset bubbles and other unintended consequences.

Although the equilibrium real rate can't be measured, it can be estimated. Figures 5 and 6 show how the equilibrium real interest rate (known as *r-star*) has evolved over the past four decades or so for the United States and for a weighted average of advanced economies in North America and Europe.[3]

These estimates show clearly that in the 2000s the equilibrium real interest rate fell from about 2.5–3 percent to somewhere between 0 percent and 0.5 percent and at times was negative. Inflation was very low as well. The Fed, the European Central Bank, and other central banks in advanced economies worried about falling into a Japanese-style deflationary spiral.

It was this understanding of how the economy had changed that led central banks to believe that they could cut interest rates aggressively, and keep them close to zero for an extended period of time, without fueling inflation. In fact, if the Fed kept interest rates at historically normal levels, it would be committing the economy to higher unemployment and dangerously low inflation. And so it cut interest rates.

Figure 5. R-Star (equilibrium real interest rate) for the United States, Laubach-Williams estimation, plotted with the trend growth rate of the US economy, a source of change that drives r-star. *Source*: Thomas Laubach and John C. Williams, "Measuring the Natural Rate of Interest," *Review of Economics and Statistics* 85, no. 4 (November 2003): 1063–70.

Figure 6. R-Star (equilibrium real interest rate) for advanced economies, Holston-Laubach-Williams estimation. Estimates are GDP-weighted averages across the United States, Canada, the Eurozone, and the United Kingdom, using OECD estimates of GDP at purchasing power parity. For dates prior to 1995, Eurozone weights are from the summed area of the eleven original Euro-area countries. *Sources*: Kathryn Holston, Thomas Laubach, and John C Williams, "Measuring the Natural Rate of Interest: International Trends and Determinants," *Journal of International Economics* 108, Supplement 1 (May 2017): S39–S75.

But when short-term interest rates were set to zero, the Fed still thought more monetary stimulus was required. In effect, it wanted to set negative short-term rates but was constrained by the zero lower bound (see chapter 3). Faced with the prospect of losing money by putting it in the bank, people may simply hold onto it. Another way to stimulate the economy is to cut longer-term interest rates. Companies often borrow over five- or ten-year horizons. Mortgages in the United States are typically fixed for thirty years. The Fed itself doesn't set longer-term interest rates. However, short-term rates affect long-term rates. Indeed, the interest rate on long-term government debt reflects expectations of future short-term rates. So current short-term rates plus an inflation target amount to "forward guidance" about the future of short-term rates and can significantly influence interest rates on longer-term government debt.

In 2008 the Fed decided these measures weren't enough and began to introduce new tools. They started to purchase long-dated securities like Treasury bonds and even privately issued debt such as mortgage-backed securities. This lowered the interest rate on these instruments, because in the world of bond arithmetic, a higher price means a lower effective yield, and vice versa. This approach was known as *quantitative easing*, or QE. These two elements of monetary policy resulted in a lot of cheap money becoming available all at once.

As Janet Yellen prepared to leave the position of Fed chair in 2017, she gave a speech in Washington, DC, stating clearly that QE, although unconventional, was part of the central bankers' tool kit in the modern era of a low r-star. "Recent studies suggest that the neutral level of the federal funds rate appears to be much lower than it was in previous decades. The bottom line is that we must recognize that our unconventional tools might have to be used again. If we are indeed living in a low-neutral-rate world, a significantly less severe economic downturn than the Great Recession might be sufficient to drive short-term interest rates back to their effective lower bound."[4]

The ultralow rates resulting from these measures had significant effects on asset prices—like housing and stocks—and on other economies, particularly those in developing countries.

CHEAP MONEY AND ASSET BUBBLES

In 2005, when she was president of the San Francisco Federal Reserve, Yellen gave a speech that offered a framework for thinking about the connection between monetary policy and asset-price bubbles.

> How, then, should monetary policy react to unusually high prices of houses—or of other assets, for that matter? . . . The debate lies in determining when, if ever, policy should be focused on deflating the asset price bubble itself.
>
> In my view, it makes sense to organize one's thinking around three consecutive questions—three hurdles to jump before pulling the monetary policy trigger. First, if the bubble were to deflate on its own, would the effect on the economy be exceedingly large? Second, is it unlikely that the Fed could mitigate the consequences? Third, is monetary policy the best tool to use to deflate a house-price bubble?
>
> My answers to these questions in the shortest possible form are, "no," "no," and "no."[5]

These remarks address an important issue for central banks in the period before ultralow interest rates and QE: when it looks as though there might be what Alan Greenspan once called "irrational exuberance" in asset markets, should central banks raise interest rates to prick those bubbles?[6] In particular, Greenspan and others were concerned about whether the low and stable inflation he had helped engineer was leading to the overvaluation of internet stocks.

Yellen was a governor of the Fed when Greenspan made this speech in December 1996. And she recounted both the Fed's stance and her implicit support of it. "The Fed suspected there was a stock price bubble developing as early as 1996. I was still at the Board when Greenspan made his famous irrational exuberance speech. The Fed chose not to try to burst the bubble. Instead, it did its very best to pick up the pieces when the bubble finally popped. I think that effort was pretty successful."[7]

The Fed took this course for a number of reasons. First, it's hard to spot a bubble in advance or to understand the motivations driving people to invest. When property prices in the San Francisco Bay Area, or Sydney, Australia, suddenly soar, is it because they are particularly nice places to live, or because people have lost touch with reality? It might have been the case that Pets.com was overvalued, but it turned out that Amazon (which went public in 1997) wasn't. Second, since bubbles tend to burst of their own accord, central banks are reluctant to risk collateral damage by intervening. Third, and perhaps most importantly, other tools can be used that might prevent bubbles forming in the first place.

In the context of housing bubbles, one of the tools available is *macro-prudential regulation*. This involves placing controls on the amount of lending in the affected sector of the economy. For instance, banks may be told by a regulator that they must require at least a 20 percent down payment for home loans or specify that loan repayments cannot exceed a certain percentage of a borrower's income. The regulator can even limit the annual rate of growth of loans.

In many ways this approach makes sense. The Tinbergen rule—named after Jan Tinbergen, the winner of the first Nobel Prize for economics—stipulates that each policy challenge requires an independent policy instrument. The Federal Open Market Committee (FOMC) is already worried about price stability and unemployment. To address these issues, it has the instruments of the federal funds rate and its communication about the future path of interest rates. Using the same tools to tackle asset bubbles is just asking for trouble.

A counterargument to this centers on the efficacy of macroprudential regulation. If macroprudential regulation isn't very effective, then it's not entirely reasonable for the FOMC or other interest-rate-setting bodies to basically say, "Somebody else is taking care of that." In fact, a reasonable body of evidence suggests that macroprudential regulation *can* be fairly effective. But there are some important caveats. For instance, a 2019 paper from the International Monetary Fund studied ninety-nine different macroprudential lending restrictions in twenty-eight European Union countries between 1990 and 2018.[8] The paper shows that although these restrictions do tend to slow the growth of credit and house prices, they take up to three years to have a meaningful effect. There is also evidence of an asymmetry in the effectiveness of measures, in the sense that stricter regulations don't do as much to curb activity as do laxer regulations in unleashing activity.

One difficulty in assessing the impact of macroprudential policies is differentiating the effects of a policy from other concurrent changes in the economy. To simply look at (say) house prices or credit growth before and after a macroprudential policy is enacted and attribute any change to that policy is to commit one of the classical logical fallacies. That is, *post hoc ergo propter hoc*, from the Latin meaning "after this therefore because of this." Modern empirical economics has developed a variety of statistical tools to address this challenge. One is the use of *instrumental variables*, for which Joshua Angrist, David Card, and Guido Imbens received the 2021 Nobel Prize in economics.[9]

In this particular setting, what one really wants is a variable that affects the likelihood of macroprudential measures being adopted but doesn't directly affect credit growth itself. A paper by the economists Niklas Gadatsch, Lukas Mann, and Isabel Schnabel proposes just that. They use the degree of political independence of macroprudential institutions in different European countries as an instrumental variable to address the causality issue. As the authors put it, their approach "is based on the idea that a politically sensitive macroprudential measure is more likely to be implemented if a politically independent institution is in charge."[10] They find that "borrower-based" measures have a meaningful effect on credit growth. In a sense this is not surprising. If a macroprudential regulation prevents somebody from getting a loan with a 10 percent down payment (perhaps requiring 15 percent or 20 percent down) when a bank was otherwise willing to make that loan, one would expect fewer loans to be made.

If macroprudential policies can be shown to affect asset prices, the bigger question is the magnitude of the effect. Do these policies put a stop to bubbles? To answer this question, one would have to know what constituted a bubble in the first place. So it's very hard to say. These policies seem to do something, but is it enough? And the even harder question is whether it's enough to warrant the FOMC or other interest-rate setting bodies effectively bracketing the question of asset-price bubbles in order to focus on their core mission, and risking inflating such bubbles in the process.

A further concern is how to respond to "irrational exuberance" in a market. If the public—or at least some meaningful portion of the public—doesn't act rationally, do central banks have a responsibility to intervene? This is a particularly important question for assets on which macroprudential regulation does not exert a clear or obvious effect. It's one thing for macroprudential policies to put the brakes on the housing market by limiting loans, but such measures would not have been effective tools for managing the dot-com bubble of the 1990s or the crypto mania of the 2020s.

The financial commentator Sebastian Mallaby argues that central banks have an obligation to focus on asset-price bubbles. He points out that "pajama-clad day-traders and boosterish financial media" were often touted as the explanation for the dot-com bubble, but that it "turned wild after a series of panicky interest-rate cuts followed the implosion of a major hedge fund in 1998" and that it finally burst after the Fed began lifting interest rates in 2000.[11] In other words, the question was always framed as whether asset-price bubbles are a monetary or a "cultural" phenomenon. Mallaby goes on to argue that once QE became part of the central banker's toolkit, there was no avoiding the issue of bubbles.

When monetary policy explicitly lowers the rate of returns on bonds and term deposits in banks, investors—even perfectly rational ones—are likely to go in search of higher yields from riskier assets, like stocks. For instance, a retired person with relatively modest and stable spending habits who suddenly finds their income halved by falling interest rates is likely to try to replace that lost income, and this requires taking on more risk. Perhaps sound financial education would alert people to these risks and to the fact that their purchasing power is not fixed, but depends on inflation-adjusted interest rates and is therefore subject to fluctuations. But one way or another, monetary policy affects risk taking in the economy. And what might appear to be rational behavior by an individual can aggregate into "irrational exuberance" at the national level.

Similarly, ultralow interest rates and the prospect that they will stay low tend to fuel growth in house prices. And because banking regulators are always at least one step behind banks, playing catch-up, there is always likely to be too much rather than too little lending in such circumstances.

That leaves interest-rate-setting bodies like the FOMC in an awkward spot. If they really confronted the facts, they would have to acknowledge that low-interest-rate policies, macroprudential regulation notwithstanding, have negative effects. But they could argue that trying to explicitly take account of the effect of monetary policy on asset prices would make matters worse. Given that data on these matters is inherently limited or absent, do we really want the Fed identifying and intervening to manage asset-price bubbles based on the intuitions of its officials? Do we want to further confuse the public about the core mission of the Fed by suggesting that it consider a broader range of issues than price stability and employment?[12]

On balance the answer to these questions has to be no. Although it's possible that the Fed and other central banks haven't contributed to asset-price bubbles with unconventional monetary policy, we need to assess the impact of this against the right counterfactual. One possible counterfactual is not to use unconventional monetary policy when faced with the zero lower bound and credit markets that are freezing up. This would have an unacceptable economic costs—particularly in terms of employment. Another possible counterfactual is that the Fed should have explicitly incorporated asset-price stability as part of their mandate. This almost by definition would have made it harder for it to achieve its goals of general price stability and employment, and the cost entailed would have far exceeded any benefits.

We should accept that central banks operate in a messy world. If there is any core lesson from looking at asset prices from 2008 to the present, it is that independent and capable macroprudential regulators are valuable and important. And those regulators don't always have the resources necessary to do their job.

THE FED'S IMPACT ON THE GLOBAL SOUTH

Most central bank policy—almost by its nature—focuses on the domestic economy. Of course the Fed takes into account what is going on in the global economy, because this affects demand for goods produced in the United States and thus can affect domestic economic conditions. In 2022 global disruptions to supply chains, resulting from the war in Ukraine and the coronavirus pandemic, increased prices for many important products, thus fueling inflation. But when the Fed sets interest rates to address its dual mandate of maintaining stable prices and employment, it takes those international factors as inputs; it doesn't consider the effects of its interest-rate policies on the rest of the world.

Yet in a globally connected world with freely and rapidly moving capital, one country's monetary policy obviously affects other countries. And the monetary policy of the United States, the largest and most important economy in the world and the issuer of the world's reserve currency, has an outsize global effect.

So in the wake of the 2008 financial crisis, when the United States and Europe responded to the reduction in the neutral rate of interest by cutting rates to zero and engaging in significant quantitative easing, these actions had a significant effect on emerging-market economies. Raghuram Rajan nailed the issue in a speech in 2014: "When monetary policy in large countries is extremely and unconventionally accommodative, capital flows into recipient countries tend to increase local leverage; this is not just due to the direct effect of cross-border banking flows but also the indirect effect, as the appreciating exchange rate and rising asset prices, especially of real estate, make it seem that borrowers have more equity than they really have."[13]

Monetary policy can affect risk taking internationally as well as in the domestic economy. When investors see low returns on offer in the United States, they look overseas for higher returns. Investing overseas also means taking on exchange-rate risk—the risk that a profitable investment could be offset or completely negated by a fall of the overseas currency against the US dollar. Nevertheless, it is clear that beginning in 2008, unconventional monetary policy in the United States drove sudden and large capital inflows into other countries.[14]

Of course, what the capital market giveth, the capital market taketh away. When a country like the US begins to unwind quantitative easing and move toward normalizing interest rates, the firehose of money that flowed into recipient countries like India reverses. Rajan made exactly this point in his speech at the Brookings Institution in 2014. (That speech, in a touch of irony, was given at the invitation of Ben Bernanke, the former Fed chair who had presided over the unconventional monetary policy of which Rajan was speaking.) "When source countries move to exit unconventional policies, some recipient countries are leveraged, imbalanced, and vulnerable to capital outflows. Given that investment managers anticipate the consequences of the future policy path, even a measured pace of exit may cause severe market turbulence and collateral damage. Indeed, the more transparent and well-communicated the exit is, the more certain the foreign investment managers may be of changed conditions, and the more rapid their exit from risky positions."[15]

There are, of course, counterarguments. Access to global capital markets is generally good for economic development, so the issue is getting the amount of inbound capital right. Surely, then, the solution is for recipient countries to use macroprudential regulation to prevent leverage from building up too quickly in their countries. This argument, however, is blind to the difficulty of pursuing macroprudential policies in a timely way. Given that plenty of wealthy countries have previously allowed large buildups of foreign capital to leave them vulnerable, it is not realistic to expect countries in the global South—often with less well-developed financial and regulatory institutions—to avoid the problem. For instance, both Ireland and Spain allowed large flows of foreign capital to inflate housing bubbles in their economies in the early 2000s, and the bursting of these bubbles was extremely disruptive both economically and socially. Rajan made this point in the same speech.

Now, the welfare of other countries is not part of the Fed's mandate. And even if it were, measuring the impact of US monetary policy on other countries would be very difficult. A more plausible remedy is greater cooperation and coordination between central banks. Rajan's speech at Brookings laid out this thinking very crisply:

> My call is for more coordination in monetary policy because I think it would be an immense improvement over the current international non-system. International monetary policy coordination, of course, is unpopular among central bankers, and I therefore have to say why I reiterate the call and what I mean by it. I do not mean that central bankers sit around a table and make policy collectively, nor do I mean that they call each other regularly and coordinate actions. In its strong form, I propose that large country central banks, both in advanced countries and emerging markets, internalize more of the spillovers from their policies in their mandate, and are forced by new

conventions on the "'rules of the game" to avoid unconventional policies with large adverse spillovers and questionable domestic benefits. . . .

Given the difficulties of operationalizing the strong form, I suggest that, at the very least, central banks reinterpret their domestic mandate to take into account other country reactions over time (and not just the immediate feedback effects), and thus become more sensitive to spillovers. This weak "coordination" could be supplemented with a reexamination of global safety nets.[16]

There has been little progress on this agenda to date. And while central banks around the world grapple with inflation shocks, it is unlikely to be a priority among central bankers. But in coming years we may well look back at Rajan's speech and wonder why, for so long, we thought that international cooperation in monetary policy was out of the question when international cooperation in other spheres of government is so important.

GOVERNMENT FINANCES AND PRINTING MONEY

During the financial crisis of 2008 and the coronavirus pandemic, central banks around the world—especially the Fed—provided extraordinary monetary stimulus. They not only lowered interest rates to zero (or below) but also bought trillions of dollars in longer-term debt securities, thereby expanding their balance sheets massively. These actions were unprecedented, but not quite as dramatic as some folks have suggested. Some commentators and pundits have claimed that current inflationary pressures are a consequence of advanced economies' "printing money" during the pandemic. These commentators often say that the United States engaged in an experiment with so-called modern monetary theory (MMT). MMT's most public proponent has been Stephanie Kelton in her book *The Deficit Myth*. [17]

There are two points to note here. First, MMT is a fringe theory that neither economists nor policymakers take seriously. Second, neither the United States nor or any other advanced economy engaged in MMT or "money printing" during the pandemic.

The United States did what any responsible government does when it wants to fund a deficit: it issued government bonds. When a government issues bonds to back a deficit, it has to convince investors that at some point, revenues will be raised or spending will be cut. Otherwise, investors won't buy the bonds at the prevailing price. And a higher price means that less deficit spending can be financed. This is the discipline of market expectations.

Now, one might counter that during the Fed's quantitative easing program, the government bonds bought by the Fed were in private hands for only a short period, typically a matter of days. It's also true that at times, the Fed was the major holder of certain government bond issues. Isn't this functionally the same as printing money? Actually, no. The fact that there is a market price for the bond—even for a short period—provides an important signal about the long-term prospects of inflation and the ability of the government to service its debt.

MMT starts with the argument that a government that can issue debt denominated in its own currency (like the United States) can always finance a budget deficit by simply electronically creating as much money as it requires. In this way, the government can never fail to make payment on US dollar–denominated liabilities. Thus the whole idea of a budget deficit is, to use Kelton's term, a "myth."

This point is neither new nor controversial: it has been accepted by central bankers, treasury officials, academic economists, and other experts for decades. But MMT proponents make a strong claim to go with this weak one: that printing money cannot lead to hyperinflation.

The important constraint facing a government is not how to cover liabilities denominated in its own currency but how to pay for real goods and services. After all, nobody cares about currency for its own sake. They care about what they can buy with that currency. In this sense, the real constraint is inflation. Indeed, the more sophisticated

MMT proponents like Kelton agree with conventional economics on this point. So the real question is, when and under what circumstances is a government likely to run into the inflation constraint?

Conventional economics outlines the circumstances under which different monetary and fiscal policy settings and different economic shocks lead to inflation—or deflation, for that matter. Although policymakers know that a country can never run out of its own currency, they nonetheless use conventional economic analysis to guide policy.

By contrast, proponents of MMT don't have much to say about when the inflation constraint will bind the government or what consequences follow if it does. Some proponents of MMT suggest that the inflation constraint cannot bind if the economy is at substantially less than full employment. According to this view, absence of inflation is a sign that the economy is below full capacity, and inflation is a sign that it is hitting capacity. But this simplistic thinking provides no guide as to how inflation interacts with the real economy when the economy is at less than full capacity. Can inflation bring down the real debt burdens of households and firms? Can inflation bring about changes in real wages even when nominal wages don't change? And if so, is that a good thing?

Perhaps more importantly, can inflation spiral out of control even when an economy is below capacity? Runaway inflation is not just a phenomenon of dysfunction or external shocks: even well-functioning economies can experience large increases in inflation when there is a structural deterioration of underlying fiscal capacity (e.g., the capacity to raise taxes or cut spending). This happened in France in the early 1980s, in New Zealand in the mid-1980s, and in both Germany and South Korea in the early 1990s.

The central problem with MMT is that there is only a finite quantity of real economic resources that can be extracted through seigniorage—the difference between the face value of physical money and its production costs. Or, to put it another way, one can only get so much lemon juice out of a lemon. In the final analysis, MMT is more wishful thinking than a coherent economic theory. It is revealing that roughly 90 percent of Kelton's book is devoted to discussing what all this extra government money could be spent on, rather than the effects of printing money.

Government Debt

Deficits aren't a myth but a reality. There are important questions about the connection between cheap money and government debts, and how sustainable those debts are.

Governments are not like households. In particular, unlike a household (or a person), governments are "infinitely lived." This means they don't ever have to pay back their debt: they just have to be able to service the debt. That is, they need to be able to make their interest payments and roll over the debt—that is, reborrow—when it comes due.

With some limited exceptions, holders of government debt don't have a secured claim on assets in the same way that a bank lending to a homeowner does.[18] The holders of government debt effectively have a claim on the ability of that government to levy taxes in order to make the payments on that debt. If there are other lenders willing to hold the debt, then the actual amount borrowed (the face value) doesn't have to be paid back. And that simply (or sometimes not so simply) relies on a belief in the ability of the government to levy those taxes and of there being a sustainable economic base from which to collect them. As Luigi Zingales, a professor of finance at the University of Chicago Booth School of Business, observed: "The crucial question that we need to figure out, is not whether we can repay the existing debt but whether we can sustain the payment of interest on a regular basis."[19]

Lenders and ratings agencies often focus of the level of a country's debt relative to the size of its economy, a measure known as *net debt to GDP*. If the amount of debt grows at a slower rate than the economy, the debt-to-GDP ratio will fall over time.[20]

How much debt is too much? There is no real formula for answering this question, although some scholars have tried to look at cross-country evidence to determine the debt-to-GDP level that causes countries to get themselves into trouble. The sustainability of debt stems from things that are hard to measure, such as investor confidence. Ultimately, it depends on what investors think is a sustainable amount of tax collection. Taxes used by the government to raise money typically reduce economic activity. There's an old adage that if you want to get less of something, you tax it. So when you tax labor supply (through income taxes), you get less of it, and when you tax employment (through payroll taxes), you get less of it.[21]

Of course, in thinking about sustainable debt capacity, governments pay particular attention to the interest rate on their debt. A reduction in the neutral interest rate enables countries to sustainably borrow more. Indeed, many economists have pointed out that when the US (or for that matter the UK or Australian or French) government can borrow long-term (say for thirty years) at a rate of less than 2 percent, and sometimes less than 1 percent, it should make large investments in physical and social infrastructure.[22] If a bridge or a new school or an optical-fiber broadband network could deliver a social rate of return of well above 2 percent, and the government can borrow at 2 percent, then it should borrow to make the investment. Many such infrastructure investments are estimated to have rates of return considerably higher than that.

So government finances are inextricably linked to the *price* of money. They are also—in an important way—linked to the *type* of money involved. Countries that issue their own currency and issue debt in that currency retain more control over their finances. So whether New Zealand can control its own currency turns out to be, at least potentially, pretty important. The question here is what the introduction of digital money might do to these prospects. But first we need to briefly think about whether a country really needs its own currency.

Economists have thought about the pros and cons of countries sharing a common currency since the early 1960s.[23] The euro represents a large-scale experiment. A common currency has some straightforward advantages. Individuals and businesses don't need to convert their money to do business between regions, so it reduces what economists call transaction costs. Imagine if the East and West Sides of New York City used different currencies, and people had to exchange bills (or carry both) to go about everyday life in the city. A common currency makes setting prices easier.

But there are downsides to a common currency as well. The first and most important is the loss of flexibility in setting interest rates. If two economic areas share a currency, the price of money is the same in both areas. And that means that monetary policy is the same—what Paul Krugman has called a "one-size-fits-all monetary policy."[24] When the Fed sets interest rates, it can't set different rates for California and Iowa, because people could move money between California and Iowa to get the better interest rate. (According to the economic concept known as the *law of one price*, the same thing has to trade for the same price in two places, otherwise I could buy it in one place and sell it in other for a riskless profit.) If the California economy is running hot, the Fed would like to raise interest rates there. And if the Iowa economy is running cold, with unemployment way too high and output well below potential, the Fed would like to cut rates in Iowa. With a common currency area this is impossible.

The United States, of course, does have a common currency, and it seems to work pretty well. Why does it work well in the United States, and why have there been problems in the Eurozone?

The economist Robert Mundell, who went on the win the Nobel Prize in economics, basically answered this question in 1961. He showed that a single currency would likely work better if the economic areas sharing that currency had labor (and other "factors of production," like capital) that could move easily between the areas. People can move from California to Iowa easily enough. And as Paul Krugman pointed out in discussing these issues, that's exactly what has happened historically in the United States.[25] In the late 1980s, Massachusetts had a large reduction in employment opportunities. If workers weren't willing to leave the state to find jobs, the only way to prevent unemployment shooting up would be for wages to fall in order to make employing Massachusetts workers more attractive. If Massachusetts had had its own currency, this could have been achieved by devaluing the "Massachusetts dollar." But there's another possibility: some workers could leave the state and get jobs elsewhere. And they did.

Another way that different economic regions within a common currency area can respond to economic shocks is through "fiscal integration."[26] The idea here is that spending by a central government could do some of the work of readjusting to the economic shock.

Obviously a central bank digital currency wouldn't change labor mobility or fiscal integration in a particular country. But a CBDC does plausibly reduce some of the transaction costs and other frictions that push in the direction of a currency union. Now, this clearly isn't going to make it sensible for different parts of New York City to have different currencies. But it does mean that some smaller countries that currently don't have their own currencies may find it feasible to do so if the currency is digitally issued. Currently eleven countries (in addition to the five US territories and the United States itself) use the US dollar as their official currency, despite the fact that sometimes these countries want very different monetary policy than they effectively inherit by using the US dollar.

The machinery involved in issuing and managing a CBDC and running an independent monetary policy is not cheap, and it may well be that little changes. But it will be interesting to see whether the growth of CBDCs also changes currency areas around the world.

8

CONCLUSION

MONEY HAS CHANGED. It has become cheaper. It has become mobile. And it is becoming digital. Cheaper money brings both opportunities and dangers. Mobile money offers the promise of greater inclusion and efficiency. And digital money could change what money can do. But with that possibility comes a fight over who will control the future of money. That's a fight between private and public interests and potentially between great powers.

If a private digital currency operator got the network-externality flywheel spinning, that currency could become the dominant means of exchange, even in a country like the United States. Facebook and the partners it had pulled together to develop libra/diem were well positioned to do just that. Two things prevented that outcome. First, Facebook's involvement in the 2016 US presidential election damaged the company's reputation, leading a number of the important partners to withdraw from the project. Second, Janet Yellen decided that the Fed would not support the libra experiment on her watch.

But if a private digital currency did become dominant, and adopted a multicurrency model as Libra proposed, then the decision about what currencies to include and what weights to assign them would be consequential. As Anup Malani and I have observed, if the private company controlling the currency did not like a particular regulatory or policy decision in a country, it could penalize that government by selling the country's currency and buying other currencies, leading to a devaluation of the first country's currency.[1] This would obviously discourage that country from taking regulatory action or a policy stance with which the private digital currency company was unhappy. In other words, countries would cede policy sovereignty—at least to some extent—to the private company.

This can't be allowed to happen. And the best way to prevent it is to create CBDCs with as many of the benefits of a private digital currency as possible. A side benefit of this option—potentially a considerable one—is that it would make unstable private cryptocurrencies much less attractive. Legendary investors, Nobel laureates, central bankers, and Yellen have all suggested that the price of bitcoin makes no sense—and perhaps they're right. But some of the demand for bitcoin—and ether in particular—is based on the promise of Web3. One doesn't have to be a wild-eyed libertarian to think that smart money and smart contracts, and possibly also decentralized autonomous organizations, will play an important role in our economic future. Right now, there's no way to make a bet on that vision other than investing in cryptocurrencies. CBDCs would be an outlet for that optimism, to the detriment of bitcoin. In other words, one of the most effective ways of regulating bitcoin would be to outcompete bitcoin.

AN INCLUSIVE FUTURE

Even though I have argued that the libra/diem proposal was a danger-ous one, many of the arguments made to support it were compelling. The billions of people around the world who are unbanked is a major problem for economic development and financial inclusion. People who are cut off from the financial system, in both developing and advanced economies, are less likely to be buffered against financial shocks, more vulnerable to theft, and less able to save for their future. The fruits of our labor are represented in money, and the lack of ability to safely store and transfer that money amounts to a lack of control over one's labor.

Viewed in this light, a CBDC might look like overkill. Can't we just give everyone a conventional bank account and a tap card? Apparently this is easier said than done, otherwise it would have happened already. There are big logistical and financial questions: Would commercial banks be subsidized by government to do this? Which ones? How large would the subsidies be?

With the introduction of a CBDC like Fedcoin, the government would have to provide everyone with access to a bank account and a tap card, at a minimum. This would enhance financial inclusion. And some thorny issues like the financial inclusion of undocumented resi-dents of the United States would likely be addressed in the process. Although the transition would involve many of the questions raised above, and would take time, there would be a clear rationale for the shift.

DOMESTIC FINANCIAL REGULATION

The promise of an inclusive future requires the US government to con-structively engage with the crypto industry. But tensions have emerged—particularly within the Democratic Party—about how to do so. On one side are Democrats like As Sen. Cory Booker (D-NJ) observed: "We are already seeing some of the hopeful, optimistic possibilities in cryptocurrency," describing it as a "democratizing" force that carries with it "a lot of hope." Another lawmaker noted that "the project of radically decentralizing the internet and finance strikes me as a profoundly progressive cause."[2]

Acknowledging these realities and opportunities, the Biden administration has sought to regulate crypto. But democratic socialists like Sen. Elizabeth Warren (D-MA) have raised obstacles to such legislation, essentially translating their inherent distrust of banks into a rigid opposition to crypto. Warren was the principal author of a letter to Secretary Yellen outlining concerns about sanctions compliance and KYC rules, stating that "we are concerned that OFAC has not developed sufficiently strong and effective procedures for enforcement in the cryptocurrency industry."[3] Warren and Sen. Sherrod Brown (D-OH) have done everything in their power to scupper the administration's attempts to regulate the crypto industry. Their position appears to be that they can best express their hostility to cryptocurrencies by refusing to regulate them. This is a profoundly counterproductive position, to put it mildly.

Constructive engagement can lead to more positive outcomes than disengagement. The United States has had great success in shaping the international discussion and agenda on a range of issues by having a seat at the table. It has advanced the interests of workers and the environment by helping shape international trade agreements rather than by cutting itself out of the process. It has promoted human rights around the world by engaging with other nations through trade as well as diplomacy.

Avoiding involvement with cryptocurrencies would have predictable results. China would step in, and the United States would not only miss out on tremendous opportunities for commerce and financial inclusion, but it would also cede effective control over the crypto landscape to China.

INTERNATIONAL FINANCIAL DIPLOMACY
AND ECONOMIC REALISM

For more than half a century, microeconomists have thought about the issues involved in being in a bilateral trading relationship where the value of that relationship can be improved by investing in it.[4] These sunk, relationship-specific investments followed by bargaining with a trading partner create the possibility of one party "holding up" the other and extracting some extra surplus from the relationship. This, in turn, deters the investments—at least to some degree—that improve the value of the relationship. The hold-up problem is central to understanding the boundaries and internal organization of firms—and the analysis of it has given rise to two Nobel Prizes, for Oliver Hart and Oliver Williamson.

In recent years it seems that the hold-up problem has gone global. We're beginning to see it play out between nations, not just firms.[5] China has exerted leverage over Australia over both iron ore and tertiary education—two of Australia's three largest export industries, for which China is by far Australia's biggest customer. For example, China has forced global suppliers to negotiate iron-ore sales through a single, state-run platform.[6] Similarly, Germany has found itself highly dependent on Russian gas supplies. And by 2022 the United States had managed to get itself into the position of buying 95 percent of its advanced microprocessors from Taiwan.

Firms have long known that vertical integration is a way to avoid hold-up. The great lesson from Oliver Hart and his coauthors Sanford Grossman and John Moore is that asset ownership confers "residual rights of control" over the assets—the right to dictate the asset's use in the case of disagreement. This outside option, or "threat point," puts the owner in a better bargaining position and hence makes relationship-specific investments more attractive.

And in the wake of pandemic-induced supply-chain disruptions, firms have moved from a "just-in-time" approach to obtaining inputs to a "just-in-case" footing. Nations are following suit. As a result of recent shortages, the United States is scrambling to establish domestic semiconductor capability. Germany is rethinking its energy strategy, and Australia is desperately trying to diversify its export customer base.

The free-trade era following World War II—which was initiated, refined, and expanded through international agreements like the General Agreement on Tariffs and Trade and international organizations like the World Trade Organization—has not and will not come to an end. But the general conduct of trade, which has emphasized commercial and economic interests and deemphasized national interests, is changing. Nation-states are expanding their role in the trade landscape, especially with respect to strategic manufacturing and strategic supply-chain management.

Money will play an important part in this changing landscape. The ability of bad actors like Vladimir Putin to hold up the rest of the world depends in no small part on an unfettered means of exchange. Measures like blocking access to the SWIFT messaging system will not be an effective way to control bad actors like this in the future. What remains to be seen is whether the replacement of SWIFT will make it easier or harder to impose sanctions and control rogue states. Widespread adoption of a digital yuan would enable China to expand and project its economic power. Conversely, the United States' ability to avoid hold-up depends on the status of the US dollar as the global reserve currency. Navigating these challenges will involve economic realism, along with an understanding that digital money will change the global economic landscape and that the winner of the CBDC race will be in an extremely powerful position.

WEB3
New Technology and Decentralized Trust

A digital future powered by CBDCs could facilitate much of the development of Web3, deal with the financial-stability risks posed by cryptocurrencies, prevent the rise of a private digital currency that could severely constrain government monetary and fiscal policy, and remove the anonymity of cash that facilitates tax evasion and illicit activities.

That's a pretty good list of benefits. But it raises the obvious question of what role, if any, will remain for cryptocurrencies. In particular, what might become of a platform like Ethereum, which has been at the forefront of Web3 developments?

As we have seen, existing cryptocurrencies consume huge amounts of energy. The economist Eric Budish shows—as a matter of logic—that decentralized trust as implemented by a proof-of-work blockchain is inherently expensive. This argument is not about the environmental costs of intensive computation per se, but about the economic resources required in general to establish and maintain decentralized trust. Budish shows that the cost of a POW consensus protocol that maintains trust has two properties:

1. The cost is large relative to the stakes involved in the trust arrangement.
2. This costly scales linearly with the trust stakes. A POW blockchain that ensures trust in something supervaluable would be supercostly.

These properties derive from three conditions that must hold to maintain decentralized trust. The first is that bitcoin mining (or its equivalent) must be in economic equilibrium. That is, "the dollar amount of compute power devoted to maintaining the trust is equal to the dollar value of compensation to miners." If this were not the case, then more miners would enter or exit mining until it was. In the first half of 2022 the cost of bitcoin mining was running at around $40 million per day.[7]

The second condition that must hold is that majority attacks must be deterred. This requires nodes controlling a majority of the computing power on the blockchain to behave honestly. But why would they behave honestly with large amounts of money to be made by not doing so? They wouldn't. So there must be a mechanism to deter anyone from acquiring more than 50 percent of the computing power of the network. In the language of economics, behaving honestly must be "incentive compatible."

The third condition connects the first two. It requires that the payments to honest nodes on the network, in the equilibrium determined by the first condition, be larger than the economic returns to behaving dishonestly and attacking the network.

Budish also shows that similar conditions obtain for proof-of-stake (POS) protocols, even if direct electricity usage is not at issue—a point also argued persuasively by Gans and Gandal.[8]

This raises two questions. First, to what degree will CBDCs reduce these costs? And second, if there are additional costs of decentralized trust, how can they be reduced?

The answer to the first question is relatively straightforward. A tokenized CBDC—or a number of CBDCs in a number of different countries that are essentially interoperable—can effectively replace bitcoin or ether as currently constituted. That is, there should and probably will be a backbone for Web3 based on the fedcoin I propose in chapter 5—that is, a tokenized, retail, central bank digital currency that is a liability of the central bank. All major countries or currency unions that have their own fiat currency today (like the Eurozone) will likely gravitate to this model if the United States adopts it.

This type of CBDC will not rely on a distributed ledger as bitcoin does. With a centralized ledger held by a country's central bank, the system would not incur the significant costs of creating decentralized trust.

Decentralized trust is an issue not only for digital currencies but also for smart contracts, which are intrinsically linked to distributed ledgers. As I've pointed out in a paper with Joshua Gans, a smart contract consists of a set of performance obligations.[9] Performance can be verified by a party (say party A) sending a message to the network. That message would contain party A's wallet address and a piece of verifiable evidence of performance of the contract. In a world of CBDCs rather than private digital currencies, the wallet address would be a CBDC wallet (with the currency specified by the contract). Under a smart contract, that transaction would then be confirmed to a block and recorded on the blockchain. At that point, a payment under the smart contract would be triggered by the receipt of the message, and tokens would be transferred to A's wallet.

If a POS protocol becomes workable, then those decentralized trust costs won't directly involve solving cryptographic problems that use up enormous amounts of energy. We will move from a protocol whereby one gets a lottery ticket on the chance to confirm a block by doing computations to a protocol whereby one gets a lottery ticket on the chance to confirm a block by locking up a bunch of tokens for a period of time. This still costs real resources, even if it doesn't involve the same environmental cost as complex computations.

Is it possible to design a protocol that reduces the cost of decentralized trust for smart contracts? In principle, yes. In another paper, Joshua Gans and I outline how to use the economic theory of mechanism design to create the appropriate incentives for people to tell the truth about what transactions should be committed to a block.[10]

This field of economics explores how strategic interactions can be designed to achieve certain outcomes. That is, if the players in a game can somehow commit to a certain game form—who the players are, the order of moves, the information available to them when they move, and the payoffs depending on what play occurs—then it might be possible to cause certain desirable outcomes to arise as an *equilibrium outcome* of that game. Eric Maskin shared the 2007 Nobel Prize in economics for his contribution to this area of research, known as implementation theory.[11] In a 1977 paper, Maskin asked: "What social outcomes can be implemented as an equilibrium of a suitably designed game form?"[12] Since then, economists have come up with a variety of different mechanisms—really game forms—that can be effective at achieving desirable outcomes. In fact, it is sometimes possible to design a game form with a unique, desirable equilibrium, and this form can be made robust to various conditions, such as some of the players not being fully rational.

Blockchain consensus and smart contracts offer rich opportunities for putting this kind of thinking to work. The whole environment is, by its very nature, "designed." And it involves specifying very clearly—in computer code—what will happen under a variety of well-defined circumstances.

Another way to put this is that appropriately designed incentives may be a way to efficiently establish decentralized trust. Even if fedcoin becomes the digital currency used as the basis of smart contracts, a consensus protocol will be required for those contracts, one that is efficient in both economic and energy-use terms. Mechanism-designed-based consensus protocols may play a useful role in this regard.

Crypto True Believers

It would be naive to think that the crypto true believers living in Keene, New Hampshire, are going to welcome fedcoin with open minds and open hearts. To them, taxes, police, and parking meters are all illegitimate impositions of government. So even if the frozen yoghurt shops in Keene that currently accept bitcoin are required under federal law to accept fedcoin, they're probably not going to like it. On the contrary, there's a fair chance that these crypto true believers will see fedcoin as a further encroachment on their freedoms. But for the great bulk of crypto enthusiasts—as opposed to fanatics—the benefits of fedcoin will likely far outweigh any perceived loss of freedom. And it is largely these enthusiasts who are pushing the development of Web3. For them, cryptocurrency is more of a tool than a religion. And fedcoin would be a vastly more useful and powerful tool than bitcoin, or even ether.

The establishment of a CBDC would remove a good deal of the heat and glamor from cryptocurrency as a speculative investment, with significant benefits for both financial stability and the economic welfare of folks who have lost bets they can't afford to lose in the Bitcoin bubble. Fedcoin would highlight what the practical and useful parts of cryptocurrency are and incorporate those into the mainstream. Bubbles will always exist: if there can be a bubble in the market for Dutch tulips, there can be a bubble in anything. But mysticism tends to contribute to bubbles. It creates a narrative of an exotic "new thing" that most people don't understand and to which investors are afforded an opportunity to get in on the ground floor. This happened with tech stocks in the late 1990s, and it has happened with cryptocurrencies. By contrast, there has basically never been a bubble in low-risk government bonds, in part because they're boring. Fedcoin has many benefits, but one of them is making cryptocurrencies a bit more boring.

THE FUTURE

I began this book by noting that the typical explanation for the exponential rise in economic progress since the mid-eighteenth century is technological progress, and that although that explanation isn't wrong, it is incomplete. Economic activity relies on both production and trade. And while technological progress can dramatically increase the productivity of an economy, capitalizing on that gain requires the ability to trade with others; and efficient trade requires a medium of exchange.

In his "irrational exuberance" speech, Alan Greenspan spoke of the centrality of money in our society: "At root, money—serving as a store of value and medium of exchange—is the lubricant that enables a society to organize itself to achieve economic progress. The ability to store the fruits of one's labor for future consumption is necessary for the accumulation of capital, the spread of technological advances and, as a consequence, rising standards of living."[13] Money will only become more central as it becomes more useful. And cheap, mobile, digital money will be more useful for more people in more settings.

Money in the twenty-first century could take many forms. But there is good reason to believe that it will represent a confluence of the visions of Buterin, Yellen, and Rajan—three experts from very different backgrounds. It will facilitate new types of economic arrangements—the core of Buterin's vision. It will—at least as far as the United States is concerned—be stable, appropriately regulated, and the world's global reserve currency. This is the core of Yellen's vision. And it will be inclusive, and more globally cooperative than before. This is the core of Rajan's vision.

Acknowledgments

I am grateful to Robert Akerlof, Rosalind Dixon, Joshua Gans, Simon Glick, Bengt Holmstrom, Greg Kaplan, and Bruce Preston for helpful discussions and comments.

I am also deeply indebted to the entire team at University of California Press. Michelle Lipinski was an exceptional and supportive editor, and I am deeply grateful to LeKeisha Hughes and Teresa Iafolla.

Notes

PROLOGUE

1. "India Loses 10Rs Lakh Crore from Black Economy Every Year," *Economic Times*, March 22, 2010.

2. Raghuram Rajan, *I Do What I Do* (New York: Harper Business, 2017), 11.

3. Rajan went on to say: "This is not just due to the direct effect of cross-border banking flows but also the indirect effect, as the appreciating exchange rate and rising asset prices, especially of real estate, make it seem that borrowers have more equity than they really have." Rajan, *I Do What I Do*, 180.

CHAPTER 1. THE YEAR THAT CHANGED EVERYTHING

1. Our World in Data, *World GDP over the Last Two Millennia*, https://ourworldindata.org/grapher/world-gdp-over-the-last-two-millennia.

2. Tobias Brunner, Guido Friebel, Richard Holden, and Suraj Prasad, "Incentives to Discover Talent," *Journal of Law, Economics and Organization*, 38, no. 2 (2022): 309–44.

3. Chapurukha Kusimba. "When—and Why—Did People First Start Using Money?" *The Conversation,* June 20, 2017, https://theconversation.com/when-and-why-did-people-first-start-using-money-78887.

4. Aristotle asserted that the first coins were minted in in Phrygia under King Midas (*Politics,* 1). Herodotus believed the Lydians were first to introduce them. Others think money was first minted on the Greek island of Aegina.

5. Barry Eichengreen, *Globalizing Capital: A History of the International Monetary System*, 3rd ed. (Princeton, NJ: Princeton University Press, 2019), 7.

6. *Apple: Steve Jobs Introduces the iPod—2001,* YouTube, www.youtube.com/watch? v=Mc_FiHTITHE.

7. Satoshi Nakamoto, *Bitcoin: A Peer-to-Peer Electronic Cash System*, Bitcoin, 2008, https://bitcoin.org/bitcoin.pdf.

8. Lawrence H. Summers. "Accepting the Reality of Secular Stagnation," *Finance & Development*, 57, no. 1 (March 2020), www.elibrary.imf.org/view/journals/022/0057/001/article-A005-en.xml.

9. Simon van Zuylen-Wood, "Ian Freeman Could Have Been a Bitcoin Billionaire. Instead He Could Go to Prison for the Rest of His Life," *New York* magazine, August 25, 2021.

10. For a detailed description, see *Bitcoin Developers Guide*, Bitcoin, n.d., https://developer.bitcoin.org/devguide/block_chain.html.

11. Tavneet Suri, "Mobile Money," Annual Review of Economics 9 (2017): 497–520; William Jack and Tavneet Suri, "Risk Sharing and Transaction Costs: Evidence from Kenya's Mobile Money Revolution," *American Economic Review* 104, no. 1 (2014): 183–223.

12. Rosalind Dixon and Richard Holden, *From Free to Fair Markets: Liberalism after COVID-19* (Oxford: Oxford University Press, 2022).

CHAPTER 2. THE CASHLESS SOCIETY

1. Raghuram Rajan, speech to the Fixed Income Money Market and Derivatives Association of India (FIMMDA), February 2014, in Raghuram Rajan, *I Do What I Do* (New York: Harper Business, 2017).

2. Friedrich Schneider, "Development of the Shadow Economy of 36 OECD Countries over 2003–2021," *African Journal of Political Science* 15, no. 2 (2021), www.fm.gov.lv/lv/media/10381/download.

3. "The Hanke-Kruse Hyperinflation Table," Cato Institute, n.d., www.cato.org/sites/cato.org/files/pubs/pdf/hanke-krus-hyperinflation-table-may-2013.pdf.

4. The classic reference on hyperinflations—which provided the commonly accepted definition of hyperinflation—is Philip Cagan, "The Monetary Dynamics of Hyperinflation," in *Studies in the Quantity Theory of Money*, ed. M. Friedman, 25–117 (Chicago: University of Chicago Press, 1956).

5. *Explore Data*, Federal Trade Commission, accessed August 1, 2023, www.ftc.gov/news-events/data-visualizations/explore-data. The FTC also reported 2.8 million cases of fraud relating to things like imposter scams and online shopping scams. See "New Data Shows FTC Received 2.8 Million Fraud Reports from Consumers in 2021," Federal Trade Commission, February 2, 2022, www.ftc.gov/news-events/news/press-releases/2022/02/new-data-shows-ftc-received-28-million-fraud-reports-consumers-2021-0. It is important to remember, however, that these did not involve like-for-like transactions such as making a purchase at a local store.

6. *Federal Bureau of Investigation Crime Data Explorer*, accessed August 1, 2023, https://cde.ucr.cjis.gov/LATEST/webapp/#/pages/home.

7. "Swish," n.d., www.swish.nu/about-swish.

8. "The New Payments Platform," Reserve Bank of Australia, n.d., www.rba.gov.au/payments-and-infrastructure/new-payments-platform.

9. "A Cashless Society," https://sweden.se/life/society/a-cashless-society.

10. Richard Holden, "How to Make Australia Cashless by 2020," *Australian Financial Review*, January 14, 2018, www.afr.com/opinion/how-to-make-australia-cashless-by-2020-20180111-hogngw.

11. *2021 FDIC Survey of Unbanked and Underbanked Households*, FDIC, www.fdic.gov/analysis/household-survey/index.html.

12. For a discussion of central network actors, such as governments, as coordination devices, see Robert Akerlof and Richard Holden, "Movers and Shakers," *Quarterly Journal of Economics*, 131, no. 4 (2016): 1849–74.

13. See Kaushik Basu, "In India, Black Money Makes for Bad Policy," *New York Times*, 27 November, 2016; *Federal Reserve Payments Study*, Federal

Reserve, updated January 14, 2022, www.federalreserve.gov/paymentsystems/december-2021-findings-from-the-federal-reserve-payments-study.htm. In 2018 and 2019 cash payments accounted for 26 percent of all payments. That figure fell to 19 percent in 2020. Some of that decline was presumably due to the pandemic and self-enforced or government-coordinated movement restrictions.

14. See C. Elgin, M. A. Kose, F. Ohnsorge, and S. Yu, *Understanding Informality*, Centre for Economic Policy Research, CERP Discussion Paper, no. 16497,2021, https://cepr.org/publications/dp16497.

15. World Bank, *World Development Indicators 2016*, April 20, 2016, https://issuu.com/world.bank.publications/docs/9781464806834? e = 0/35179276.

16. "Full Text: PM Modi's 2016 Demonetisation Speech That Shocked India," *Business Standard,* updated November 8, 2017.

17. Jagdish Bhagwati, Pravin Krishna, and Suresh Sundaresan, "War on Black Money: Demonetisation Is a Courageous Reform That Will Bring Substantive Benefits," *Times of India*, December 14, 2016.

18. Manish Singh, "The Ugly Face of India's Demonetization," Mashable, November 16, 2016, https://mashable.com/article/india-people-dying-demonetization.

19. Wade Shepard, "One Month In, What's the Impact of India's Demonetization Fiasco?" *Forbes*, December 12, 2016.

20. Rajan, *I Do What I Do.*

21. Rajan, *I Do What I Do.*

22. Rajesh Ahuja and Sreyasi Pal, "Demonetisation 100 Days: Fake Rs 2000 Notes Entering India through Bangladesh," *Hindustan Times*, February 16, 2017.

23. Wade Shepard, "How India Is Surviving Post-demonetization," *Forbes*, July 29, 2017.

CHAPTER 3. MOBILE MONEY AND DIGITAL BANKING

1. "Remarks by the President in Nominating Dr. Janet Yellen as Chair of the Board of Governors of the Federal Reserve System," White House, October 9, 2013, https://obamawhitehouse.archives.gov/the-press-office/2013/10/09/remarks-president-nominating-dr-janet-yellen-chair-board-governors-feder.

2. The classic economic model of bank runs appears in Douglas W. Diamond and Philip H. Dybvig, "Bank Runs, Deposit Insurance, and Liquidity," *Journal of Political Economy*, 91, no. 3 (1983): 401–19.

3. Janet Yellen, "Challenges Confronting Monetary Policy," speech at National Association for Business Economics Policy Conference, Washington, DC, March 4, 2013, www.federalreserve.gov/newsevents/speech/yellen20130302a.htm.

4. Adriane Jeffries, "Apple Pay Allows You to Pay at the Counter with Your iPhone 6," The Verge, September 10, 2014, www.theverge.com/2014/9/9/6084211 /apple-pay-iphone-6-nfc-mobile-payment.

5. Asli Demirgüç-Kunt, Leora Klapper, Dorothe Singer, and Saniya Ansar, *Financial Inclusion, Digital Payments, and Resilience in the Age of COVID-19* (Washington, DC: World Bank Group, 2021), http://documents.worldbank.org /curated/en/099833507072223098/IDUof917b4120aa0f042270bbd10c8b257c99a54.

6. Tavneet Suri, "Mobile Money," *Annual Review of Economics* 9 (2017): 497–520.

7. GSM Association, *State of the Industry Report on Mobile Money*, 2022, www .gsma.com/sotir/wp-content/uploads/2022/03/GSMA_State_of_the_Industry_ 2022_English.pdf.

8. Suri, "Mobile Money."

9. William Jack and Tavneet Suri, "Risk Sharing and Transactions Costs: Evidence from Kenya's Mobile Money Revolution," *American Economic Review* 104, no. 1 (2014): 183–223.

10. See Tavneet Suri, William Jack, and Thomas M. Stoker, "Documenting the Birth of a Financial Economy," *PNAS* 109, no. 26 (2012): 10257–62.

11. Tavneet Suri and William Jack, "The Long-Run Poverty and Gender Impacts of Mobile Money," *Science* 354, no. 6317 (2016): 1288–92.

12. See Diem Association, *Vision*, n.d., www.diem.com/en-us/vision.

CHAPTER 4. CRYPTO

1. Satoshi Nakamoto, *Bitcoin: A Peer-to-Peer Electronic Cash System*, Bitcoin, 2008, https://bitcoin.org/bitcoin.pdf.

2. Ben S. Bernanke, "The Subprime Mortgage Market," speech at the Federal Reserve Bank of Chicago's 43rd Annual Conference on Bank Structure and Competition, Chicago, May 17 2007, www.federalreserve.gov/newsevents /speech/bernanke20070517a.htm.

3. I believe this remark originated with the MIT economist and Nobel laureate Bengt Holmstrom.

4. Nakamoto, *Bitcoin*.

5. Joshua. S. Gans and Neil Gandal, "Consensus Mechanisms for the Blockchain," in *The Palgrave Handbook of Technological Finance*, ed. Raghavendra Rau, Robert Wardrop, and Luigi Zingales, 269–86 (N.p. : Palgrave Macmillan Cham, 2021).

6. See Richard Holden and Anup Malani, *Can Blockchain Solve the Hold-Up Problem in Contracts?* (Cambridge: Cambridge University Press, 2021).

7. For a detailed discussion—and proposed resolution to—forking on blockchains, see Joshua S. Gans and Richard Holden, *Mechanism-Design Approaches to Blockchain Consensus*, National Bureau of Economic Research, NBER Working Paper, no. 30189, 2022, http://www.nber.org/papers/w30189.

8. Nakamoto, *Bitcoin*.

9. Nakamoto, *Bitcoin*.

10. A hash function (hence the term *hashing*) is a type of one-way mathematical function, which Anup Malani and I defined as follows:

> A one-way function is a function where if you know the inputs, you can produce the outputs, but if you only have the outputs, you cannot know for sure the inputs. . . . An example is $2 + 3 = 5$. The inputs are 2 and 3 and the function is addition. The output is 5. If you know 2 and 3, you know the output of addition is 5. But if you know only 5, you cannot know whether the inputs are 2 and 3 or any of the following pairs: (0,5), (5,0), (1,4), (4,1), (3,2). Addition is not the best one-way function for blockchain. A better example than addition is prime factorization, which is actually used in cryptography. If I give you number X and ask you the fewest number of primes that, when multiplied together, yield X, you have a problem that rises quickly in complexity as X increases. If I tell you a series of primes, you can easy calculate its product X; but if I just give you X, it is very difficult to calculate its prime factorization.

Holden and Malani, *Can Blockchain Solve the Hold-Up Problem?*, 29.

11. Morgan Peck, "The Uncanny Mind That Built Ethereum," *Wired*, June 13, 2016.

12. Vitalik Buterin, *Ethereum: A Next-Generation Smart Contract and Decentralized Application Platform*, Ethereum, 2014, https://ethereum.org/669c9e2e20 27310b6b3cdce6e1c52962/Ethereum_Whitepaper_-_Buterin_2014. pdf.

13. Buterin, *Ethereum*.

14. Buterin, *Ethereum*.

15. See, for instance, Oliver Hart, *Firms, Contracts, and Financial Structure*, (Oxford: Clarendon Press, 1995).

16. Buterin, *Ethereum*.

17. Study of the implications of hold-up has given rise to two Nobel Prizes in Economic Sciences—to Oliver Williamson in 2009 and Oliver Hart in 2016.

18. As we note: "Economists have designed a number of contracting solutions—called mechanisms– to tackle the hold-up problem. The logic behind these mechanisms stem from the observation that if this renegotiation could be structured differently, then perhaps the social optimum could be obtained despite hold-up." Holden and Malani, *Can Blockchain Solve the Hold-Up Problem?*, 8.

19. See Nicolas Vega, "Warren Buffett Wouldn't Buy 'All of the Bitcoin in the World' for $25: 'It Doesn't Produce Anything,'" CNBC, May 2, 2022, www .cnbc.com/2022/05/02/warren-buffett-wouldnt-spend-25-on-all-of-the-bitcoin-in-the-world.html.

20. "Yellen Sounds Warning about 'Extremely Inefficient' Bitcoin," CNBC, February 22, 2021, www.cnbc.com/2021/02/22/yellen-sounds-warning-about-extremely-inefficient-bitcoin.html.

21. Paul Krugman. "Technobabble, Libertarian Derp, and Bitcoin," *New York Times*, May 20, 2021.

22. Paul Krugman. "Transaction Costs and Tethers: Why I'm a Crypto Skeptic," *New York Times*, July 31, 2018.

23. "Cryptocurrencies," Chicago Booth, July 31, 2019, www.igmchicago .org/surveys/cryptocurrencies.

24. "Cryptocurrencies."

25. Jacob Bernstein, "What Can You Actually Buy with Bitcoin?" *New York Times*, February 3, 2021.

26. See "In Defense of Bitcoin Maximalism," Vitalik Buterin's Website, April 1, 2022, https://vitalik.ca/general/2022/04/01/maximalist.html.

27. "Phial of Galadriel," Tolkien Gateway, n.d., http://tolkiengateway.net /wiki/Phial_of_Galadriel.

28. See "Market Share of the Leading Ride-Hailing Companies in the United States from September 2017 to July 2021," Statista, September 22, 2022, www.statista.com/statistics/910704/market-share-of-rideshare-companies-united-states.

29. Robert Akerlof, Richard Holden, and Luis Rayo. "Network Externalities and Market Dominance," *Management Science*, forthcoming.

30. "Bitcoin Transaction Volume Surpasses American Express," Cointelegraph, 1 February, 2022, https://cointelegraph.com/news/bitcoin-network-transaction-volume-surpasses-american-express-research.

31. Olga Kharif, "Bitcoin's Dominance of Crypto Payments is Starting to Erode," *Time*, January 16, 2022.

32. "ACH Network Seeks 29.1 Billion in Payments in 2021," Nacha, February 3, 2022, www.nacha.org/news/ach-network-sees-291-billion-payments-2021-led-major-gains-b2b-and-same-day-ach.

33. Edward de Bono, *The IBM Dollar*, Centre for the Study of Financial Innovation, 1994, www.debono.com/_files/ugd/acf405_39837dc2de76488aa91dea51a1021c31. pdf.

34. Libra Association, "An Introduction to Libra," revised July 23, 2019, https://sls.gmu.edu/pfrt/wp-content/uploads/sites/54/2020/02/LibraWhitePaper_en_US-Rev0723. pdf.

35. For an excellent summary of the economics of stable coins, see Christian Catalini, Alonso de Gortari, and Nihar Shah, "Some Simple Economics of Stable Coins," *Annual Review of Financial Economics* 14 (2022), www.annualreviews.org/doi/pdf/10.1146/annurev-financial-111621–101151.

36. Libra Association, "An Introduction to Libra," 5.

37. See Joshua S. Gans and Richard Holden, *Mechanism-Design Approaches to Blockchain Consensus*, National Bureau of Economic Research, NBER Working Paper, no. 30189, 2022, http://www.nber.org/papers/w30189; M. Pease, R. Shostak, and L. Lamport, "Reaching Agreement in the Presence of Faults," *Journal of the ACM* 27, no. 2 (1980): 228–34; Ethan Buchman, "Tendermint: Byzantine Fault Tolerance in the Age of Blockchains," PhD diss., University of Guelph, 2016; Vitalik Buterin and Virgil Griffith, "Casper the Friendly Finality Gadget," Arxiv preprint, 2017, https://arxiv.org/abs/1710.09437.

38. Libra Association, "An Introduction to Libra," 7.

39. Libra Association, "An Introduction to Libra," 7.

40. Libra Association, "An Introduction to Libra," 7.

41. Libra Association, "An Introduction to Libra," 7.

42. David Yaffe-Bellany, "The Coin That Could Wreck Crypto." *New York Times*, June 17, 2022.

43. See Testimony of Secretary of the Treasury Janet L. Yellen before the Committee on Financial Services, US House of Representatives, May 12, 2022, https://home.treasury.gov/news/press-releases/jy0776.

44. Testimony of Secretary of the Treasury Janet L. Yellen, May 12, 2022.

45. Steven Ehrlich, "Crypto's Crash Broke the Buck for TerraUSD," *Forbes*, May 10, 2022.

46. Libra Association, "An Introduction to Libra," 8.

47. Libra Association, "An Introduction to Libra," 8.

48. Libra Association, "An Introduction to Libra," 8.

49. Joshua S. Gans and Hanna Halaburda, "Some Economics of Private Digital Currencies," in *Economic Analysis of the Digital Economy*, ed. Avi Goldfarb, Shane M. Greenstein, and Catherine E. Tucker, 257–76 (Chicago: University of Chicago Press, 2015).

50. As shown in Akerlof, Holden, and Rayo, "Network Externalities and Market Dominance," services like Amazon Prime change the impulse of consumers. This doesn't mean that consumers will necessarily buy from the supplier with whom they have the impulse, but it does play a role in selecting between different equilibria in a coordination game in markets with network externalities. An increase in a dominant firm's impulse also leads to higher prices and lower consumer and total surplus.

51. These included EBay, Stripe, Mastercard, Visa and Mercado Pago. "Facebook's Libra Cryptocurrency Coalition Is Falling Apart as eBay, Visa, Mastercard, and Stripe Jump Ship," CNBC, October 11, 2019, www.cnbc.com/2019/10/11/ebay-drops-out-of-facebook-libra-cryptocurrency-one-week-after-paypal.html.

52. See "Facebook Currency Chief Faces Withering Questioning from Democrats in Congress," CNBC, July 17, 2019, www.cnbc.com/2019/07/17/facebook-currency-chief-questioned-at-house-financial-services-hearing.html.

53. For video footage of the exchange, see Carole Cadwalladr (@carolecadwalla), "Be Still My Beating Heart," Twitter, October 24, 2019, https://twitter.com/carolecadwalla/status/1187095903368351745?s=20&t=oVNrmtR3VpcBq99–4-zcFg.

54. "Visa Statement on Involvement in the Libra Association," Visa, October 12, 2019, https://usa.visa.com/visa-everywhere/blog/bdp/2019/10/11/visa-update-1570828991831. html.

55. See "ESPN Explores Sports-Betting Deal Worth At Least $3 Billion, " *Wall Street Journal*, August 27, 2021.

56. For all the requirements listed here, see Investment Company Institute, *Summary of Key Money Market Fund Regulatory Requirements*, September 28, 2016, www.ici.org/mmfs/current/16_mmf_reg_summ.

57. See "Online Marketplaces in Japan," Webretailer, updated June 13, 2023, www.webretailer.com/b/online-marketplaces-japan.

58. Richard Holden and Anup Malani, "An Examination of Velocity and Initial Coin Offerings," *Management Science* 68, no. 12 (2022): 9026–41.

59. "$257 Million: Filecoin Breaks All-Time Record for ICO Funding," Coindesk, September 8, 2017, www.coindesk.com/257-million-filecoin-breaks-time-record-ico-funding.

60. "Filecoin Token Sale Economics,"Coinlist, accessed August 2, 2023, https://coinlist.co/assets/index/filecoin_2017_index/Filecoin-Sale-Economics-e3f703f8cd5f644aecd7ae3860ce932064ce014dd60de115d67ff1e9047ffa8e.pdf.

61. See Richard Holden and Anup Malani, "The Law and Economics of Blockchain," *Annual Review of Law and Social Sciences* 18 (2022): 297–313.

62. See Richard Holden and Anup Malani, "Why the I.R.S. Fears Bitcoin," *New York Times*, January 22, 2018.

63. Holden and Malani, "Why the I.R.S. Fears Bitcoin."

64. "Swiss Bank Pleads Guilty in Manhattan Federal Court to Conspiracy to Evade Taxes," press release, United States Attorney for the Southern Districts, January 3, 2013, www.justice.gov/usao-sdny/pr/swiss-bank-pleads-guilty-manhattan-federal-court-conspiracy-evade-taxes.

65. See "Voluntary Disclosure," The Tax Lawyer, n.d., www.thetaxlawyer.com/voluntary-disclosure.

66. Paul Krugman, "How Crypto Became the New Subprime," *New York Times*, January 27, 2022.

67. Lael Brainard, "Crypto-Assets and Decentralized Finance through a Financial Stability Lens," speech at Bank of England Conference, London, July 8, 2022.

68. Brainard, "Crypto-Assets and Decentralized Finance."

69. Brainard, "Crypto-Assets and Decentralized Finance."

70. See President's Working Group on Financial Markets, the Federal Deposit Insurance Corporation and the Office of the Comptroller of the Currency,

Report on Stablecoins. November 2021, https://home.treasury.gov/system /files/136/StableCoinReport_Nov1_508. pdf: "To address additional concerns about systemic risk and concentration of economic power, legislation should require stable coin issuers to comply with activities restrictions that limit affiliation with commercial entities. Supervisors should have authority to implement standards to promote interoperability among stable coins. In addition, Congress may wish to consider other standards for custodial wallet providers, such as limits on affiliation with commercial entities or on use of users' transaction data."

71. *Greenhouse Gas Equivalencies Calculator,* Environmental Protection Agency, n.d., www.epa.gov/energy/greenhouse-gases-equivalencies-calculator-calculations-and-references.

72. *Bitcoin Network Power Demand*, Cambridge Bitcoin Electricity Consumption Index, n.d. https://ccaf.io/cbnsi/cbeci.

73. A substantially more detailed and complete treatment appears in Vitalik Buterin, "A Proof of Stake Design Philosophy," Medium, December 30, 2106, https://medium.com/@ VitalikButerin/a-proof-ofstake-design-philosophy-506585978d51.

74. See "Ethereum's Energy Usage Will Soon Decrease by ~99.95%," Ethereum Foundation blog, May 18, 2021, https://blog.ethereum.org/2021/05/18/ country-power-no-more. To put this change in perspective, the post notes: "In total, a Proof-of-Stake Ethereum therefore consumes something on the order of 2.62 megawatt. This is not on the scale of countries, provinces, or even cities, but that of a small town (around 2100 American homes)."

75. Robert Akerlof and Richard Holden, "Movers and Shakers," *Quarterly Journal of Economics* 131, no. 4 (2016): 1849–74.

CHAPTER 5. GOVCOINS

1. Janet Yellen, "Remarks from Secretary of the Treasury Janet L. Yellen on Digital Assets," speech at American University Kogod School of Business Center for Innovation, April 7, 2022, https://home.treasury.gov/news/press-releases /jy0706.

2. See "Simplifying Life with Easy Finances," Island Pay, n.d., https:// islandpay.com/personal.

3. Bank for International Settlements, *Ithanon-LionRock to mBridge: Building a Multi CBDC Platform for International Payments*, September 28, 2021, www.bis .org/publ/othp40. htm.

4. Bank for International Settlements, "Multi-CBDC Prototype Shows Potential for Reducing Costs and Speeding Up Cross-Border Payments," press release, 28 September 2021, www.bis.org/press/p210928. htm.

5. Bank for International Settlements, *Ithanon-LionRock to mBridge*.

6. A partial but remarkable list, compiled by the *New York Times*, included the following sectors and companies.

> Consumer goods and retail: Adidas, British American Tobacco, Canada Goose, Uniqlo, H&M, Ikea, Nestlé, Nike, TJX, and Unilever
>
> Energy: BP, Exxon Mobil, and Shell
>
> Finance: American Express, Bank of America, BNY Mellon, Citigroup, Deutsche Bank, Goldman Sachs, JPMorgan Chase, Mastercard, Visa, Société Générale, Western Union, and Zurich Insurance Group
>
> Food: Carlsberg, Heineken, Little Caesars, Mars, McDonalds, PepsiCo, Restaurant Brands International, Starbucks, and Yum Brands
>
> Media: Bloomberg, Netflix, the Walt Disney Company, and Warner Bros.
>
> Professional Services: Bain, BCG, McKinsey, Deloitte, EY, KPMG, and PwC
>
> Tech: Amazon Web Services, Apple, Cogent, Ericsson, Google, IBM, Intel, LG Electronics, Lumen, Nokia, Microsoft, SAP, Sony, and Uber
>
> Travel and logistics: Marriott, Airbus, Amadeus, American Airlines, Boeing, Delta, Hyatt, Hilton, FedEx, DHL, Sabre, United Airlines, and UPS
>
> Manufacturing: Caterpillar, Hitachi, Michelin, Renault, Siemens, Stelantis, Tata Steel, and Volvo

"Companies are Getting Out of Russia, Sometimes at a Cost," *New York Times,* October 14, 2022.

7. SWIFT noted that "in 2022 (March and June), pursuant to international and multilateral action to intensify financial sanctions against Russia, specialised financial messaging providers, such as Swift, were prohibited from providing services to designated entities under EU Council Regulation (EU) 833/2014. As Swift is incorporated under Belgian law and must comply with EU regulation, Swift disconnected all designated Russian entities (and their designated Russia-

based subsidiaries) from the Swift network. Additionally, in compliance with EU Council Regulation (EU) 765/2006 containing similar prohibition, Swift also disconnected designated Belarusian entities (and their designated Belarus-based subsidiaries)." Swift, "Compliance: Swift and Sanctions?," n.d., www.swift.com /about-us/legal/compliance-0/swift-and-sanctions#what-is-swift?

8. A very helpful discussion, on which the following treatment draws heavily, is Hanna Armelius, Gabriela Guibourg, Stig Johansson, and Johan Schmalholz, "E-krona Design Models: Pros, Cons and Trade-offs," *Sveriges Riksbank Economic Review* 2020 (2): 80–96.

9. Armelius et al., "E-krona Design Models," offers a useful description of how a decentralized ledger would work in the Swedish setting with both a regular currency and an e-krona:

> Intermediaries, called nodes in the network in the distributed ledger technology (DLT) terminology, exchange central bank reserves in their RIX accounts for newly issued e-kronor assigned to their wallet/vault . . . . End-users exchange the desired amount of e-krona through an intermediary by decreasing the same amount in their commercial bank deposits followed by a deposit onto their e-krona accounts/ wallets. . . . The customer pays for goods or services from a merchant with e-kronor and thus the customer's e-krona account/wallet is decreased by this amount while the merchant's e-krona holdings increase by the same amount . . . . If the merchant does not want to increase their e-krona holdings, they can exchange the received amount of e-krona for increased bank deposits through their intermediary . . . . The intermediary can either accept the increase of e-krona holdings or exchange these for central bank reserves at the central bank through RIX. In that case, the Riksbank redeems e-kronor in the same way as currently is done with physical cash.

10. See US Federal Reserve, *Money and Payments: The U.S. Dollar in the Age of Digital Transformation*, January, 2022, www.federalreserve.gov/publications /files/money-and-payments-20220120. pdf.

11. Markus K. Brunnermeier and Dirk Niepelt, "On the Equivalence of Private and Public Money," *Journal of Monetary Economics* 106 (2019): 28.

12. That is not to say that there have not been concerns voiced about this issue. A Fed discussion paper summarizes them as follows:

> Banks currently rely (in large part) on deposits to fund their loans. A widely available CBDC would serve as a close—or, in the case of an interest-bearing CBDC,

near-perfect—substitute for commercial bank money. This substitution effect could reduce the aggregate amount of deposits in the banking system, which could in turn increase bank funding expenses, and reduce credit availability or raise credit costs for households and businesses. Similarly, an interest-bearing CBDC could result in a shift away from other low-risk assets, such as shares in money market mutual funds, Treasury bills, and other short-term instruments. A shift away from these other low-risk assets could reduce credit availability or raise credit costs for businesses and governments. These concerns could potentially be mitigated by CBDC design choices. A non-interest-bearing CBDC, for example, would be less attractive as a substitute for commercial bank money. In addition, a central bank might limit the amount of CBDC an end user could hold.

US Federal Reserve, *Money and Payments.*

13. See, for instance, Armelius et al., "E-krona Design Models."

14. Milton Friedman, *Counter-revolution in Monetary Theory*, Institute of Economic Affairs, Occasional Paper 33, 1970.

15. Raghuram Rajan, speech to the Fixed Income Money Market and Derivatives Association of India (FIMMDA), February 2014, reprinted in Raghuram Rajan, *I Do What I Do* (New York: Harper Business. 2017).

16. Polly Sprenger, "Sun on Privacy: 'Get Over It,'" *Wired*, 26 January, 1999, www.wired.com/1999/01/sun-on-privacy-get-over-it.

17. Samuel Warren and Louis Brandeis, "The Right to Privacy," *Harvard Law Review* 4, no. 5 (December 1890): 193–220.

18. The First Amendment guarantees privacy of beliefs. The Third Amendment protects the privacy of one's home (against demands that it be used to house soldiers). The Fourth Amendment protects individuals and their possessions against unreasonable searches and seizures. And the Fifth Amendment. which provides protection against self-incrimination, protects the privacy of one's own information.

19. The former Fed chair Ben Bernanke has made this analogy. See Ben S. Bernanke, *21st Century Monetary Policy* (New York: W. W Norton, 2022), 496.

20. Even if there was (meaningful) competition between a private and a public currency, then this would also have an impact. Economists have analyzed models of currency competition. One such model assumes that the central bank follows an inflation-targeting regime (as many central banks currently do) but that the cryptocurrency just seeks growth in what amounts

to market share. Such a situation has important implications for monetary policy. If the supply or price of the cryptocurrency changes, then the central bank needs to inject its own fiat currency into the money supply to meet its inflation target. See Linda Schilling and Harald Uhlig, "Some Simple Bitcoin Economics," *Journal of Monetary Economics* 106 (2019): 16–26.

21. See Citi Treasury and Trade Solutions, *The Regulated Internet of Value*, Citi, n.d., https://icg.citi.com/rcs/icgPublic/storage/public/2031240-Regulated-Internet-Value.pdf.

CHAPTER 6. THE EXORBITANT PRIVILEGE

1. Committee on the Global Financial System, "US Dollar Funding: An International Perspective," June 2020, www.bis.org/publ/cgfs65. pdf.

2. Janet Yellen, "Remarks from Secretary of the Treasury Janet L. Yellen," American University Kogod School of Business Center for Innovation, April 7, 2022.

3. Barry Eichengreen, *Exorbitant Privilege: The Rise and Fall of the Dollar and the Future of the International Monetary System* (Oxford: Oxford University Press. 2011).

4. Charles P. Kindleberger, "Dominance and Leadership in the International Economy: Exploitation, Public Goods, and Free Rides," *International Studies Quarterly* 25, no 2 (1981): 242–54.

5. These benefits have been nicely elucidated by the leading scholar of these issues, Helene Rey. See, for instance, "Global Financial Cycles," David Finch Lecture, University of Melbourne, 2019, www.youtube.com/watch? v= 8LfiVfh7748.

6. See Ben S. Bernanke, "The Dollar's International Role: An 'Exorbitant Privilege'?" Brookings Institution blog, January 7, 2016, www.brookings .edu/blog/ben-bernanke/2016/01/07/the-dollars-international-role-an-exorbitant-privilege-2.

7. See Zefeng Chen, Zhengyang Jiang, Hanno Lustig, Stijn Van Nieuwerburgh, and Mindy Z. Xiaolan, "Exorbitant Privilege Gained and Lost: Fiscal Implications." unpublished paper, www.gsb.stanford.edu/faculty-research /working-papers/exorbitant-privilege-gained-lost-fiscal-implications: "As predicted by theories of safe asset determination, investors concentrate extra fiscal capacity in a single country, the global safe asset supplier, based on relative

macro fundamentals, and its debt growth may temporarily outstrip what is warranted by its own macro fundamentals."

8. Bernanke, The Dollar's International Role."

9. In "The Dollar's International Role," Bernanke used the terminology of network externalities, noting that "people are accustomed to using the dollar in international transactions, and the willingness of others to take dollars increases their usefulness (economists call this a 'network externality')."

10. Robert Akerlof, Richard Holden, and Luis Rayo, "Network Externalities and Market Dominance," *Management Science*, forthcoming, shows how inertia, in the sense of "impulses," can lead to a dominant competitor staying "in" (or dominant) in markets with network externalities. There, impulses involve a fairly weak form of inertia, in that they are level-0 beliefs in a cognitive hierarchy model where the level of thinking (and hence iterated best responses to other player's lower-level best responses) is taken to infinity.

11. Bruce Ackerman, *We the People,* vol. 2, *Transformations* (Cambridge, MA: Harvard University Press, 1998).

12. Niles Eldredge and Stephen Jay Gould, "Punctuated Equilibria: An Alternative to Phyletic Gradualism," in *Models in Paleobiology*, ed. J. M. Schopf, 82–115 (Baltimore, MD: Johns Hopkins University Press, 1972). This comparison to Akerman's work is made explicitly in Walter Dean Burnham, "Constitutional Moments and Punctuated Equilibria: A Political Scientist Confronts Bruce Ackerman's 'We the People,'" *Yale Law Journal* 108, no. 8 (1999): 2237–77.

13. Raymond Zhong, "Australia Bars China's Huawei From Building 5G Wireless Network," *New York Times*, August 23, 2018.

14. Chris Buckley, "After Years of Acrimony, China and Australia Cautiously Reach Out," *New York Times*, June 24, 2022.

15. See Richard Holden and Anup Malani, *Can Blockchain Solve the Hold-Up Problem in Contracts?* (Cambridge: Cambridge University Press, 2021).

16. See, for instance, Andre R. Jaglom and Michael W. Galligan, "New York Law as the Gold Standard Choice," New York State Bar Association, November, 1, 2019, https://nysba.org/new-york-law-as-the-gold-standard-choice-for-global-business-contracts.

17. "U.S. Treasury Sanctions Nearly 100 Targets in Putin's War Machine, Prohibits Russian Gold Imports," press release, US Department of the Treasury, June 28, 2022, https://home.treasury.gov/news/press-releases/jy0838.

18. "U.S. Treasury Sanctions Nearly 100 Targets."

19. Jonathan Schanzer and Emanuele Ottolenghi, "Turkey's Teflon Don," *Foreign Policy*, March 31, 2014.

20. "The Reports of the Corruption Scandal Involving the Names of the Former Ministers of the AKP Were Published on the Internet," Cumhuriyet, March 14, 2014, www.cumhuriyet.com.tr/haber/fezlekeleri-indirmek-icin-tiklayin-50525.

21. Schanzer and Ottolenghi, "Turkey's Teflon Don."

22. Schanzer and Ottolenghi, "Turkey's Teflon Don."

23. Jonathan Schanzer, "The Biggest Sanctions-Evasion Scheme in Recent History," *The Atlantic*, January 5, 2018.

24. The six planks included the following specific provisions:

This action will freeze any of Sberbank's and Alfa Bank's assets touching the U.S financial system and prohibit U.S. persons from doing business with them. . . . .

President Biden will sign a new Executive Order (E.O.) that includes a prohibition on new investment in Russia by U.S. persons wherever located, which will further isolate Russia from the global economy. This action builds on the decision made by more than 600 multinational businesses to exit from Russia. . . .

This will prohibit any U.S. person from transacting with these entities and freeze any of their assets subject to U.S. jurisdiction, thereby damaging the Kremlin's ability to use these entities it depends on to enable and fund its war in Ukraine. . . .

[These sanctions applied to individuals, including] President Putin's adult children, Foreign Minister Lavrov's wife and daughter, and members of Russia's Security Council including former President and Prime Minister of Russia Dmitry Medvedev and Prime Minister Mikhail Mishustin. . . .

Sanctions do not preclude payments on Russian sovereign debt at this time, provided Russia uses funds outside of U.S. jurisdiction. However, Russia is a global financial pariah—and it will now need to choose between draining its available funds to make debt payments or default. . . .

As we continue escalating our sanctions and other economic measures against Russia for its brutal war against Ukraine, we reiterate our commitment to exempting essential humanitarian and related activities that benefit the Russian people and people around the world: ensuring the availability of basic foodstuffs and agricultural commodities, safeguarding access to medicine and medical devices, and enabling telecommunications services to support the flow of information and access to the internet which provides outside perspectives to the Russian people.

"Fact Sheet: United States, G7 and EU Impose Severe and Immediate Costs on Russia," White House, April 6, 2022, www.whitehouse.gov/briefing-room /statements-releases/2022/04/06/fact-sheet-united-states-g7-and-eu-impose-severe-and-immediate-costs-on-russia.

25. "Beijing's New Digital Yuan Test Features ATMs That Convert Digital Currency to Cash," The Block, February 18, 2021, www.theblock.co/post /95266/beijing-digital-yuan-cash-atm.

26. Robert Greene, *What Will Be the Impact of China's State-Sponsored Digital Currency?* Carnegie Endowment for Peace, 2021, https://carnegieendowment. org/2021/07/01/what-will-be-impact-of-china-s-state-sponsored-digital-currency-pub-84868.

27. "China is a large country with vast territory, large population, multiple ethnic groups and wide differences in regional development. In such a society, people's payment habits, age and security needs vary. Therefore, physical RMB enjoys advantages that could not be replaced by other means of payment." Working Group on E-CNY Research and Development of the People's Bank of China, *Progress of Research and Development of E-CNY in China*, July 2021, www .pbc.gov.cn/en/3688110/3688172/4157443/4293696/2021071614584691871. pdf.

28. Adam Cohen, *The Perfect Store: Inside eBay* (Boston: Back Bay Books, 2021).

29. Zhou Xin, "China Digital Currency: e-CNY rollouts Expand to Hang-zhou and Chongqing as Chinese Central Bank Seeks Broad Support for Its Push to Go Cashless," *South China Morning Post*, April 2, 2022.

30. Enoch Yiu, "Hong Kong Sets Stage for e-CNY Use, to Launch Pilot 'Soon After Spring Festival,'" *South China Morning Post*, February 7, 2022.

31. Working Group on E-CNY Research and Development of the People's Bank of China, *Progress of Research and Development*.

32. Working Group on E-CNY Research and Development of the People's Bank of China, *Progress of Research and Development*. The statement goes on to say: "As digital technology and electronic payment develop, the use of cash in retail payments has been on a decline. However, it's the mandate of the central bank to ensure the public's direct access to cash, and make sure the unit of account is consistent in the era of digital economy by digitalizing cash."

33. See Working Group on E-CNY Research and Development of the People's Bank of China, *Progress of Research and Development.*

34. Raymond Zhong, "In Halting Ant's I.P.O., China Sends a Warning to Business," *New York Times*, November 6, 2020.

35. Robert Olsen, "Jack Ma's Alibaba Hit with $2.8 Billion Fine for Abusing Its Dominant Market Position," *Forbes*, April 10, 2021.

36. Working Group on E-CNY Research and Development of the People's Bank of China, *Progress of Research and Development.*

37. As the PBOC has noted: "Some believe that retail CBDC is more attractive than deposits and may lead to financial disintermediation, narrow banking, and credit squeeze, while others argue that easy availability of CBDC can enhance the transmission of policy rates to the money and credit markets. If CBDC bears interest at a relatively attractive level, institutional investors might move from low-risk assets such as short-term government securities to CBDC, which will have an impact on the price of these assets." Working Group on E-CNY Research and Development of the People's Bank of China, *Progress of Research and Development.*

CHAPTER 7. CHEAP MONEY, ASSET BUBBLES, AND GOVERNMENT FINANCES

1. The average from November 1960 to December 2007 was 6.12 percent.

2. *Playbook Deep Dive*, Politico, podcast, July 22, 2022, https://podcasts.apple.com/us/podcast/playbook-deep-dive/id1111319839? i = 1000570787184.

3. "Measuring the Natural Rate of Interest," Federal Reserve Bank of New York, updated May 19, 2023, www.newyorkfed.org/research/policy/rstar.

4. Janet L. Yellen, "A Challenging Decade and a Question for the Future," Herbert Stein Memorial Lecture, National Economists Club, Washington, DC, October 20, 2017, www.federalreserve.gov/newsevents/speech/yellen20171020a.htm.

5. Janet L. Yellen, "Housing Bubbles and Monetary Policy," speech at the Fourth Annual Haas Gala, San Francisco, CA, October 21, 2005, www.frbsf.org/our-district/press/presidents-speeches/yellen-speeches/2005/october/housing-bubbles-and-monetary-policy.

6. See Alan Greenspan, "The Challenge of Central Banking in a Democratic Society," Francis Boyer Lecture of the American Enterprise Institute

for Public Policy Research, Washington, DC, December 5, 1996, www .federalreserve.gov/boarddocs/speeches/1996/19961205. htm.

7. Yellen, "Housing Bubbles and Monetary Policy."

8. See Tigran Poghosyan, *How Effective is Macroprudential Policy? Evidence from Lending Restriction Measures in EU Countries*, IMF Working Paper, no. 2019 /045. March 1, 2019, www.imf.org/en/Publications/WP/Issues/2019/03/01/How-Effective-is-Macroprudential-Policy-Evidence-from-Lending-Restriction-Measures-in-EU-46640.

9. "Prize in Economic Sciences 2021," press release, Nobel Prize, 11 October, 2021, www.nobelprize.org/prizes/economic-sciences/2021/press-release.

10. Niklas Gadatsch, Lukas Mann, and Isabel Schnabel, "A New IV Approach for Estimating the Efficacy of Macroprudential Measures," *Economics Letters* 168 (2018): 107–9.

11. Sebastian Mallaby, "Can the Fed Pop Bubbles before They Go Bad?" *Washington Post*, May 16, 2022.

12. Elsewhere I have written extensively about the problems arising from the Reserve Bank of Australia (RBA)'s targeting asset prices and the exchange rate in addition to price stability and employment. Exactly in accordance with the Tinbergen rule, this has created problems when these variables provide conflicting predictions about interest rates. And by obscuring the focus on price stability, this practice has made it harder for the RBA to maintain credibility regarding inflation expectations. See, for example, Richard Holden, "RBA Has Got Interest Rates More Right Than Wrong," *Australian Financial Review*, February 8, 2022.

13. Raghuram Rajan, *I Do What I Do* (New York: Harper Business, 2017), 180.

14. Rajan, *I Do What I Do*, 181.

15. Raghuram Rajan, "Competitive Monetary Easing—Is It Yesterday Once More?," speech at the Brookings Institution, Washington DC, April 10, 2014, www.bis.org/review/r140414b.htm.

16. Rajan, "Competitive Monetary Easing."

17. Stephanie Kelton, *The Deficit Myth* (New York: Hachette, 2020).

18. One exception that is in equal parts amusing, concerning, and instructive is the case of Argentina and the distressed debt fund Elliot Capital. As the *Washington Post* reported, the fund tried to seize various Argentinian assets in order to collect on a decade-old debt.

Elliott Capital's arguably most audacious scheme came in 2012, when the Argentine Navy's proud three-masted tall ship pulled into the port of Tema in Ghana with more than 250 crew members on board, recent graduates of the Escuela Naval de Argentina participating in an annual training session. The *Libertad* was worth a fraction of what the hedge fund claimed that it was owed, but the 100-meter ship quickly became a chip in an international fight over billions in old debt. Elliott Capital persuaded a Ghanaian court to seize the vessel so it could collect on its debt. Argentinian officials would lash out at Elliott as "unscrupulous financiers" and after more than two months the ship was released."

Renae Merle, "How One Hedge Fund Made $2 Billion from Argentina's Economic Collapse," *Washington Post.* March 29, 2016.

19. "Coronavirus: How Are We Going to Pay for It?," podcast, Capitalisn't, April 17, 2020, www.chicagobooth.edu/review/capitalisnt-coronavirus-how-are-we-going-pay-it.

20. See Olivier Blanchard, "Public Debt and Low Interest Rates," *American Economic Review* 109, no. 4 (2019): 1197–1229; Chris Edmond, Richard Holden, and Bruce Preston, "Should We Worry about Government Debt?" *Australian Economic Review* 53, no. 4 (2020): 557–65.

21. An exception to the point that taxes are distortionary are so-called Pigouvian taxes, named after the British economist Arthur Pigou, who first wrote about them in 1913. Pigouvian taxes are designed to "internalize externalities" into the price mechanism and thus make sure that the market-clearing role that the price mechanism plays in equilibrating supply and demand in a given market takes account of the social cost of activities not otherwise included in market prices. The classic example is pollution of various kinds, and the leading application is a carbon tax to balance the environmental costs and the economic benefits of carbon dioxide emissions.

22. See, for example, Paul Krugman, "Time to Borrow," *New York Times*, August 8, 2016; Lawrence Summers, "The Next President Should Make Infrastructure Spending a Priority," *Washington Post*, September 11, 2016; Richard Holden, "Big Project Spending a Good Way to Kickstart Stagnant Economy," *Australian Financial Review*, August 19, 2015.

23. See Robert Mundell, "A Theory of Optimum Currency Areas," *American Economic Review* 51, no. 4 (1961): 657–65.

24. Paul Krugman, "Revenge of the Optimum Currency Area," *NBER Macroeconomics Annual* 27, no. 1 (2013): 439–48.

25. Krugman, "Revenge of the Optimum Currency Area."

26. See Peter Kenen, "The Theory of Optimum Currency Areas: An Eclectic View," in *Monetary Problems of the International Economy*, ed R. Mundell and A. Swoboda, 41–60 (Chicago: University of Chicago Press, 1969).

CHAPTER 8. CONCLUSION

1. Richard Holden and Anup Malani, "The Law and Economics of Blockchain," *Annual Review of Law and Social Sciences* 18 (2022): 297–313.

2. Quoted in Zachary Warmbrodt, "Elizabeth Warren's Anti-crypto Crusade Splits the left," Politico, 15 March, 2022, www.politico.com/news/2022/03/15/democrats-divided-crypto-future-00015804.

3. See letter to the Honorable Janet Yellen from Senators Elizabeth Warren, Mark R. Warner, Sherrod Brown, and Jack Reed, March 2, 2002, www.warren.senate.gov/imo/media/doc/2022.03.01% 20Letter% 20to% 20Treasury% 20re% 20OFAC% 20crypto% 20sanctions% 20enforcement.pdf.

4. Classic references include: Benjamin Klein, "Vertical Integration as Organizational Ownership: The Fisher Body–General Motors Relationship Revisited," *Journal of Law, Economics, and Organization* 4 (1988): 199–213; Oliver E. Williamson, *Markets and Hierarchies, Analysis and Antitrust Implications: A Study in the Economics of Internal Organization* (New York: Free Press, 1975).

5. See Richard Holden, "Supply Chain Issues No Justification for Economic Nationalism," *Australian Financial Review*, April 20, 2022.

6. Eric Gluyas, "China's Iron Ore Platform Could Spark a Shift in Pricing Power," *Australian Financial Review*, February 22, 2022.

7. Eric B. Budish, *The Economic Limits of Bitcoin and Anonymous, Decentralized Trust on the Blockchain*, University of Chicago, Becker Friedman Institute for Economics Working Paper, No. 83, 2022, https://papers.ssrn.com/sol3/papers.cfm? abstract_id = 4148014.

8. Budish, *The Economic Limits of Bitcoin*; Joshua. S. Gans and Neil Gandal, "Consensus Mechanisms for the Blockchain." in *The Palgrave Handbook of Technological Finance,* ed. Raghavendra Rau, Robert Wardrop, and Luigi Zingales, 269–86. (N.p. : Palgrave Macmillan Cham, 2021). As Budish puts it: "In its sim-

plest form, proof-of-stake is vulnerable to exactly the same critique . . . as proof-of-work. Just conceptualize c as the rental cost of stake (i.e., the opportunity cost of locking up one unit of the cryptocurrency), as opposed to the rental cost of capital plus variable electricity cost of running the capital. The amount of stake that will be locked up for validation will depend on the compensation to stakers . . . . This amount of stake in turn determines the level of security against majority attack . . . . Thus . . . the per-block compensation to stakers [needs] to be large relative to the value of a majority attack."

9. See Joshua S. Gans and Richard Holden, *A Solomonic Solution to Ownership Disputes: An Application to Blockchain Frontrunning*, National Bureau of Economic Research, NBER Working Paper, no. 29780, 2022, www.nber.org/papers/w29780.

10. Joshua S. Gans and Richard Holden, *Mechanism-Design Approaches to Blockchain Consensus*, National Bureau of Economic Research, NBER Working Paper, no. 30189, 2022, www.nber.org/papers/w30189.

11. "The Sveriges Riksbank Prize in Economic Sciences in Memory of Alfred Nobel 2007," Nobel Prize, n.d., www.nobelprize.org/prizes/economic-sciences/2007/summary.

12. Eventually published as Eric Maskin, "Nash Equilibrium and Welfare Optimality," *Review of Economic Studies* 66, no. 1 (1999): 23–38.

13. Alan Greenspan, "The Challenge of Central Banking in a Democratic Society," Francis Boyer Lecture, American Enterprise Institute for Public Policy Research, Washington, DC, December 5, 1996, www.federalreserve.gov/boarddocs/speeches/1996/19961205. htm.

References

2021 FDIC Survey of Unbanked and Underbanked Households, FDIC. www.fdic.gov/analysis/household-survey/index.html.

"$257 Million: Filecoin Breaks All-Time Record for ICO Funding." Coindesk. September 8, 2017. www.coindesk.com/257-million-filecoin-breaks-time-record-ico-funding.

"ACH Network Seeks 29.1 Billion in Payments in 2021." Nacha. February 3, 2022. www.nacha.org/news/ach-network-sees-291-billion-payments-2021-led-major-gains-b2b-and-same-day-ach.

Ahuja, Rajesh, and Sreyasi Pal. "Demonetisation 100 Days: Fake Rs 2000 Notes Entering India through Bangladesh." *Hindustan Times*. February 16, 2017.

Akerlof, Robert, and Richard Holden. "Movers and Shakers." *Quarterly Journal of Economics* 131, no. 4 (2016): 1849–74.

Akerlof, Robert, Richard Holden, and Luis Rayo. "Network Externalities and Market Dominance." *Management Science*. Forthcoming.

Armelius, Hanna, Gabriela Guibourg, Stig Johansson, and Johan Schmalholz. "E-krona Design Models: Pros, Cons and Trade-Offs." *Sveriges Riksbank Economic Review* 2020, no. 2: 80–96.

Bank for International Settlements. *Ithanon-LionRock to mBridge: Building a Multi CBDC Platform for International Payments*. September 28, 2021. www.bis.org/publ/othp40. htm.

———. "Multi-CBDC Prototype Shows Potential for Reducing Costs and Speeding Up Cross-Border Payments." Press release. 28 September 2021. www.bis.org/press/p210928. htm.

Basu, Kaushik. "In India, Black Money Makes for Bad Policy." *New York Times*. November 27, 2016.

"Beijing's New Digital Yuan Test Features ATMs That Convert Digital Currency to Cash." The Block. February 18, 2021. www.theblock.co/post/95266/beijing-digital-yuan-cash-atm.

Bernanke, Ben S. *21st Century Monetary Policy*. New York: W. W. Norton, 2022.

———. "'Audit the Fed' Is Not about Auditing the Fed." Brookings Institution blog. January 11, 2016. www.brookings.edu/blog/ben-bernanke/2016/01/11/audit-the-fed-is-not-about-auditing-the-fed.

———. "The Dollar's International Role: An 'Exorbitant Privilege'?" Brookings Institution blog. January 7, 2016, www.brookings.edu/blog/ben-bernanke/2016/01/07/the-dollars-international-role-an-exorbitant-privilege-2.

———. "The Subprime Mortgage Market." Speech at the Federal Reserve Bank of Chicago's 43rd Annual Conference on Bank Structure and Competition, Chicago, May 17 2007, www.federalreserve.gov/newsevents/speech/bernanke20070517a.htm.

Bernstein, Jacob. "What Can You Actually Buy with Bitcoin?" *New York Times*. February 3, 2021.

Bhagwati, Jagdish, Pravin Krishna, and Suresh Sundaresan. "War on Black Money: Demonetisation Is a Courageous Reform That Will Bring Substantive Benefits." *Times of India*. December 14, 2016.

Bitcoin Developers Guide. Bitcoin. n.d. https://developer.bitcoin.org/devguide/block_chain.html.

Bitcoin Network Power Demand. Cambridge Bitcoin Electricity Consumption Index. n.d. https://ccaf.io/cbnsi/cbeci.

"Bitcoin Transaction Volume Surpasses American Express." Cointelegraph. 1 February,2022.https://cointelegraph.com/news/bitcoin-network-transaction-volume-surpasses-american-express-research.

Blanchard, Olivier. "Public Debt and Low Interest Rates." *American Economic Review* 109, no. 4 (2019): 1197–1229.

Brainard, Lael. "Crypto-assets and Decentralized Finance through a Financial Stability Lens." Speech at Bank of England Conference, London. July 8, 2022. www.federalreserve.gov/newsevents/speech/brainard20220708a.htm.

Brunner, Tobias, Guido Friebel, Richard Holden, and Suraj Prasad. "Incentives to Discover Talent." *Journal of Law, Economics and Organization*, 38, no. 2 (2022): 309–44.

Brunnermeier, Markus K., and Dirk Niepelt. "On the Equivalence of Private and Public Money." *Journal of Monetary Economics* 106 (2019): 27–41.

Buchman, Ethan. "Tendermint: Byzantine Fault Tolerance in the Age of Blockchains." PhD diss., University of Guelph, 2016.

Buckley, Chris. "After Years of Acrimony, China and Australia Cautiously Reach Out." *New York Times.* June 24, 2022.

Budish, Eric B. *The Economic Limits of Bitcoin and Anonymous, Decentralized Trust on the Blockchain.* University of Chicago, Becker Friedman Institute for Economics, Working Paper No. 83, 2022. https://papers.ssrn.com/sol3/papers.cfm? abstract_id = 4148014.

Burnman, Walter Dean. "Constitutional Moments and Punctuated Equilibria: A Political Scientist Confronts Bruce Ackerman's 'We the People.'" *Yale Law Journal* 108, no. 8 (1999): 2237–77.

Buterin, Vitalik. *Ethereum: A Next-Generation Smart Contract and Decentralized Application Platform.* Ethereum. 2014. https://ethereum.org/669c9e2e2027310 b6b3cdce6e1c52962/Ethereum_Whitepaper_-_Buterin_2014. pdf.

———. "A Proof of Stake Design Philosophy." Medium. December 30, 2016. https://medium.com/@VitalikButerin/a-proof-ofstake-design-philosophy-506585978d51.

———. "Slasher: A Punitive Proof-of-Stake Algorithm." 2014. https://blog.ethereum.org/2014/01/15/slasher-a-punitive-proof-of-stake-algorithm.

Buterin, Vitalik, and Virgil Griffith. "Casper the Friendly Finality Gadget." ArXiv preprint. 2017. https://arxiv.org/abs/1710.09437.

Cagan, Philip. "The Monetary Dynamics of Hyperinflation." In *Studies in the Quantity Theory of Money,* edited by M. Friedman, 25–117. Chicago: University of Chicago Press, 1956.

Carleton, Tamma, and Michael Greenstone. *Updating the United States Government's Social Cost of Carbon*. University of Chicago, Becker Friedman Institute for Economics Working Paper, no. 2021–04. January 14, 2021.

"A Cashless Society." https://sweden.se/life/society/a-cashless-society.

Catalini, Christian, Alonso de Gortari, and Nihar Shah. "Some Simple Economics of Stable Coins." *Annual Review of Financial Economics* 14 (2022). www.annualreviews.org/doi/pdf/10.1146/annurev-financial-111621–101151.

Chen, Zefeng, Zhengyang Jiang, Hanno Lustig, Stijn Van Nieuwerburgh, and Mindy Z. Xiaolan. "Exorbitant Privilege Gained and Lost: Fiscal Implications." Unpublished paper. 2022. www.gsb.stanford.edu/faculty-research/working-papers/exorbitant-privilege-gained-lost-fiscal-implications.

Citi Treasury and Trade Solutions. *The Regulated Internet of Value*. Citi. n.d. https://icg.citi.com/rcs/icgPublic/storage/public/2031240-Regulated-Internet-Value.pdf. Cohen, Adam. *The Perfect Store: Inside eBay*. Boston: Back Bay Books, 2003.

Committee on the Global Financial System. "US Dollar Funding: An International Perspective." June 2020. www.bis.org/publ/cgfs65. pdf.

"Companies are Getting Out of Russia, Sometimes at a Cost." *New York Times*. October 14, 2022.

"Coronavirus: How Are We Going to Pay for It?" Podcast, Capitalisn't. April 17, 2020. www.chicagobooth.edu/review/capitalisnt-coronavirus-how-are-we-going-pay-it.

"Cryptocurrencies." Chicago Booth. July 31, 2019. www.igmchicago.org/surveys/cryptocurrencies.

De Bono, Edward. *The IBM Dollar*. Centre for the Study of Financial Innovation, 1994. www.debono.com/_files/ugd/acf405_39837dc2de76488aa91dea51a1021c31. pdf.

Demirgüç-Kunt, Asli, Leora Klapper, Dorothe Singer, and Saniya Ansar. *Financial Inclusion, Digital Payments, and Resilience in the Age of COVID-19*. Washington, DC: World Bank Group, 2021. http://documents.worldbank.org/curated/en/099833507072223098/IDU0f917b4120aa0f04227obbd10c8b257c99a54.

Diamond, Douglas W., and Philip H. Dybvig. "Bank Runs, Deposit Insurance, and Liquidity." *Journal of Political Economy*, 91, no. 3 (1983): 401–19.

Diem Association. *Vision*. n.d. www.diem.com/en-us/vision.

Dixon, Rosalind, and Richard Holden. *From Free to Fair Markets: Liberalism after COVID-19*. Oxford: Oxford University Press, 2022.

Edmond, Chris, Richard Holden, and Bruce Preston. "Should We Worry about Government Debt?" *Australian Economic Review* 53, no. 4 (2020): 557–65.

Ehrlich, Steven. "Crypto's Crash Broke the Buck for TerraUSD." *Forbes*. May 10, 2022.

Eichengreen, Barry. *Exorbitant Privilege: The Rise and Fall of the Dollar and the Future of the International Monetary System*. Oxford: Oxford University Press, 2011.

———. *Globalizing Capital: A History of the International Monetary System*. 3rd ed. Princeton, NJ: Princeton University Press, 2019.

Eldredge, Niles, and Stephen Jay Gould. "Punctuated Equilibria: An Alternative to Phyletic Gradualism." In *Models in Paleobiology*, edited by J. M. Schopf, 82–115. Baltimore, MD: Johns Hopkins University Press, 1972.

Elgin, C., M. A. Kose, F. Ohnsorge, and S. Yu. *Understanding Informality*. CERP Discussion Pape, no. 16497, Centre for Economic Policy Research, London, 2021.

"ESPN Explores Sports-Betting Deal Worth At Least $3 Billion. "*Wall Street Journal*. August 27, 2021.

"Ethereum's Energy Usage Will Soon Decrease by ~99.95%." Ethereum Foundation blog. May 18, 2021. https://blog.ethereum.org/2021/05/18/country-power-no-more.

Explore Data. Federal Trade Commission. www.ftc.gov/news-events/data-visualizations/explore-data.

"Facebook Currency Chief Faces Withering Questioning from Democrats in Congress." CNBC. July 17, 2019. www.cnbc.com/2019/07/17/facebook-currency-chief-questioned-at-house-financial-services-hearing.html.

"Facebook's Libra Cryptocurrency Coalition Is Falling Apart as eBay, Visa, Mastercard, and Stripe Jump Ship." CNBC. October 11, 2019. www.cnbc.com/2019/10/11/ebay-drops-out-of-facebook-libra-cryptocurrency-one-week-after-paypal.html.

Federal Bureau of Investigation Crime Data Explorer. https://cde.ucr.cjis.gov/LATEST/webapp/#/pages/home.

Federal Reserve Payments Study. Federal Reserve. Updated January 14, 2022. www.federalreserve.gov/paymentsystems/december-2021-findings-from-the-federal-reserve-payments-study.htm.

"Filecoin Token Sale Economics." Coinlist. https://coinlist.co/assets/index/filecoin_2017_index/Filecoin-Sale-Economics-e3f703f8cd5f644aecd7ae3860ce932064ce014dd60de115d67ff1e9047ffa8e.pdf, accessed August 2, 2023.

Friedman, Milton. *Counter-revolution in Monetary Theory.* Institute of Economic Affairs, Occasional Paper 33, 1970.

"Full Text: PM Modi's 2016 Demonetisation Speech That Shocked India." *Business Standard.* Updated November 8, 2017.

Gadatsch, Niklas, Lukas Mann, and Isabel Schnabel. "A New IV Approach for Estimating the Efficacy of Macroprudential Measures." *Economics Letters* 168 (2018): 107–9.

Gans, Joshua. S., and Neil Gandal. "Consensus Mechanisms for the Blockchain." In *The Palgrave Handbook of Technological Finance,* edited by Raghavendra Rau, Robert Wardrop, and Luigi Zingales, 269–86. N.p. : Palgrave Macmillan Cham, 2021.

Gans, Joshua S., and Hanna Halaburda. "Some Economics of Private Digital Currencies." In *Economic Analysis of the Digital Economy,* edited by Avi Goldfarb, Shane M. Greenstein, and Catherine E. Tucker, 257–76. Chicago: University of Chicago Press, 2015.

Gans, Joshua S., and Richard Holden. *Mechanism-Design Approaches to Blockchain Consensus.* National Bureau of Economic Research, NBER Working Paper, no. 30189, 2022. www.nber.org/papers/w30189.

———. *A Solomonic Solution to Ownership Disputes: An Application to Blockchain Frontrunning.* National Bureau of Economic Research, NBER Working Paper, no. 29780, 2022. www.nber.org/papers/w29780.

Gluyas, Eric. "China's Iron-Ore Platform Could Spark a Shift in Pricing Power." *Australian Financial Review.* February 22, 2022.

Greene, Robert. *What Will Be the Impact of China's State-Sponsored Digital Currency?* Carnegie Endowment for Peace, 2021. https://carnegieendowment.org/2021/07/01/what-will-be-impact-of-china-s-state-sponsored-digital-currency-pub-84868.

Greenhouse Gas Equivalencies Calculator. Environmental Protection Agency. n.d. www.epa.gov/energy/greenhouse-gases-equivalencies-calculator-calculations-and-references.

Greenspan, Alan. "The Challenge of Central Banking in a Democratic Society." Francis Boyer Lecture, American Enterprise Institute for Public Policy Research, Washington, DC, December 5, 1996. www.federalreserve.gov/boarddocs/speeches/1996/19961205. htm.

GSM Association. *State of the Industry Report on Mobile Money.* 10th ed. 2022. www.gsma.com/sotir/wp-content/uploads/2022/03/GSMA_State_of_the_Industry_2022_English.pdf.

"The Hanke-Kruse Hyperinflation Table." Cato Institute. n.d. www.cato.org/sites/cato.org/files/pubs/pdf/hanke-krus-hyperinflation-table-may-2013.pdf.

Hart, Oliver. *Firms, Contracts, and Financial Structure.* Oxford: Clarendon Press, 1995.

Holden, Richard. "Big Project Spending a Good Way to Kickstart Stagnant Economy." *Australian Financial Review.* August 19, 2015. www.afr.com/policy/big-project-spending-a-good-way-to-kickstart-stagnant-economy-20150819-gj2i7v.

————. "How to Make Australia Cashless by 2020." *Australian Financial Review.* January 14, 2018. www.afr.com/opinion/how-to-make-australia-cashless-by-2020–20180111-hogngw.

————. "RBA Has Got Interest Rates More Right Than Wrong." *Australian Financial Review.* February 8, 2022. www.afr.com/policy/economy/rba-s-has-got-interest-rates-more-right-than-wrong-20220207-p59uhc.

————. "Supply Chain Issues No Justification for Economic Nationalism." *Australian Financial Review.* April 20, 2022. www.afr.com/policy/economy/supply-chain-issues-no-justification-for-economic-nationalism-20220419-p5aebg.

Holden, Richard, and Anup Malani. *Can Blockchain Solve the Hold-Up Problem in Contracts?* Cambridge: Cambridge University Press, 2021.

————. "An Examination of Velocity and Initial Coin Offerings." *Management Science* 68, no. 12 (2022): 9026–41.

————. "The Law and Economics of Blockchain." *Annual Review of Law and Social Sciences* 18 (2022): 297–313.

————. "Why the I.R.S. Fears Bitcoin." *New York Times.* January 22, 2018.

Holston, Kathryn, Thomas Laubach, and John C Williams. "Measuring the Natural Rate of Interest: International Trends and Determinants." *Journal of International Economics* 108, Supplement 1 (May 2017): S39–S75.

"In Defense of Bitcoin Maximalism." Vitalik Buterin's Website. April 1, 2022. https://vitalik.ca/general/2022/04/01/maximalist.html.

"India Loses 10Rs Lakh Crore from Black Economy Every Year." *Economic Times.* March 22, 2010.

Investment Company Institute. *Summary of Key Money Market Fund Regulatory Requirements*. September 28, 2016. www.ici.org/mmfs/current/16_mmf_reg_summ.

Jack, William, and Tavneet Suri. "Risk Sharing and Transactions Costs: Evidence from Kenya's Mobile Money Revolution." *American Economic Review* 104, no. 1 (2014): 183–223.

Jaglom, Andre R., and Michael W. Galligan. "New York Law as the Gold Standard Choice." New York State Bar Association. November, 1, 2019. https://nysba.org/new-york-law-as-the-gold-standard-choice-for-global-business-contracts.

Jeffries, Adriane. "Apple Pay Allows You to Pay at the Counter with Your iPhone 6." The Verge. September 10, 2014, www.theverge.com/2014/9/9/6084211/apple-pay-iphone-6-nfc-mobile-payment.

Kenen, Peter. "The Theory of Optimum Currency Areas: An Eclectic View." In *Monetary Problems of the International Economy*, edited by R. Mundell and A. Swoboda, 41–60. Chicago: University of Chicago Press, 1969.

Kharif, Olga. "Bitcoin's Dominance of Crypto Payments is Starting to Erode." *Time*. January 16, 2022.

Kindleberger, Charles P. "Dominance and Leadership in the International Economy: Exploitation, Public Goods, and Free Rides." *International Studies Quarterly* 25, no. 2. 1981: 242–54.

Klein, Benjamin. "Vertical Integration as Organizational Ownership: The Fisher Body–General Motors Relationship Revisited." *Journal of Law, Economics, and Organization* 4 (1988): 199–213.

Krugman, Paul. "Crypto is Crashing. Where Were the Regulators?" *New York Times*. July 11, 2022.

———. "How Crypto Became the New Subprime." *New York Times*. January 27, 2022.

———. "Revenge of the Optimum Currency Area." *NBER Macroeconomics Annual* 27, no. 1. 2013: 439–48.

———. "Technobabble, Libertarian Derp, and Bitcoin." *New York Times*. May 20, 2021.

———. "Time to Borrow." *New York Times*. August 8, 2016.

———. "Transaction Costs and Tethers: Why I'm a Crypto Skeptic." *New York Times*. July 31, 2018.

Kusimba, Chapurukha. "When—and Why—Did People First Start Using Money?" The Conversation. June 20, 2017. https://theconversation.com/when-and-why-did-people-first-start-using-money-78887.

Libra Association. "An Introduction to Libra." Revised July 23, 2019. Available at https://sls.gmu.edu/pfrt/wp-content/uploads/sites/54/2020/02/LibraWhite Paper_en_US-Rev0723. pdf.

Laubach, Thomas, and John C. Williams. "Measuring the Natural Rate of Interest." *Review of Economics and Statistics* 85, no. 4 (November 2003): 1063–70.

Mallaby, Sebastian. "Can the Fed Pop Bubbles before They Go Bad?" *Washington Post*. May 16, 2022.

Maskin, Eric. "Nash Equilibrium and Welfare Optimality." *Review of Economic Studies* 66, no. 1 (1999): 23–38.

"Measuring the Natural Rate of Interest." Federal Reserve Bank of New York. Updated May 19, 2023. www.newyorkfed.org/research/policy/rstar.

Merle, Renae. "How One Hedge Fund Made $2 Billion from Argentina's Economic Collapse." *Washington Post*. March 29, 2016.

Mundell, Robert. "A Theory of Optimum Currency Areas." *American Economic Review* 51, no. 4 (1961): 657–65.

Nakamoto, Satoshi. *Bitcoin: A Peer-to-Peer Electronic Cash System*. Bitcoin. 2008. https://bitcoin.org/bitcoin.pdf.

"New Data Shows FTC Received 2.8 Million Fraud Reports from Consumers in 2021." Federal Trade Commission. February 2, 2022. www.ftc.gov/news-events/news/press-releases/2022/02/new-data-shows-ftc-received-28-million-fraud-reports-consumers-2021.

"The New Payments Platform." Reserve Bank of Australia. n.d. www.rba.gov .au/payments-and-infrastructure/new-payments-platform.

Olsen, Robert. "Jack Ma's Alibaba Hit with $2.8 Billion Fine for Abusing Its Dominant Market Position." *Forbes*. April 10, 2021.

"Online Marketplaces in Japan." Webretailer. Updated June 13, 2023. www .webretailer.com/b/online-marketplaces-japan.

Our World in Data. *World GDP over the Last Two Millennia*. n.d. https:// ourworldindata.org/grapher/world-gdp-over-the-last-two-millennia.

Pease, M., R. Shostak, and L. Lamport. "Reaching Agreement in the Presence of Faults." *Journal of the ACM* 27, no. 2 (1980): 228–34.

Peck, Morgan. "The Uncanny Mind That Built Ethereum." *Wired*. June 13, 2016.

"Phial of Galadriel." Tolkien Gateway, n.d. http://tolkiengateway.net/wiki/Phial_of_Galadriel.

Poghosyan, Tigran. *How Effective Is Macroprudential Policy? Evidence from Lending Restriction Measures in EU Countries*. IMF Working Paper, 2019/045. March 1, 2019. www.imf.org/en/Publications/WP/Issues/2019/03/01/How-Effective-is-Macroprudential-Policy-Evidence-from-Lending-Restriction-Measures-in-EU-46640.

"Prize in Economic Sciences 2021." Press release, Nobel Prize. 11 October, 2021, www.nobelprize.org/prizes/economic-sciences/2021/press-release.

Rajan, Raghuram. "Competitive Monetary Easing—Is It Yesterday Once More?" Speech at the Brookings Institution, Washington DC, April 10, 2014. www.bis.org/review/r140414b.htm.

———. *I Do What I Do*. New York: Harper Business, 2017.

"Remarks by the President in Nominating Dr. Janet Yellen as Chair of the Board of Governors of the Federal Reserve System." White House. October 9, 2013. https://obamawhitehouse.archives.gov/the-press-office/2013/10/09/remarks-president-nominating-dr-janet-yellen-chair-board-governors-feder.

"The Reports of the Corruption Scandal Involving the Names of the Former Ministers of the AKP Were Published on the Internet" (in Turkish). Cumhuriyet. March 14, 2014. www.cumhuriyet.com.tr/haber/fezlekeleri-indirmek-icin-tiklayin-50525.

Rey, Helene. "Global Financial Cycles." David Finch Lecture, University of Melbourne, 2019. www.youtube.com/watch? v=8LfiVfh7748.

Saleh, Fahad. "Blockchain without Waste: Proof-of-Stake." *Review of Financial Studies* 34 (2021): 1156–90.

Schanzer, Jonathan. "The Biggest Sanctions-Evasion Scheme in Recent History." *The Atlantic*. January 5, 2018.

Schanzer, Jonathan, and Emanuele Ottolenghi. "Turkey's Teflon Don." *Foreign Policy*. March 31, 2014.

Schilling, Linda, and Harald Uhlig. "Some Simple Bitcoin Economics." *Journal of Monetary Economics* 106 (2019): 16–26.

Schneider, Friedrich. "Development of the Shadow Economy of 36 OECD Countries over 2003–2021." *African Journal of Political Science* 15, no. 2 (2021). www.fm.gov.lv/lv/media/10381/download.

Shapiro, Walter. "1989–2001: America's Long Lost Weekend." *New Republic*. June 27, 2022.

Shepard, Wade. "How India is Surviving Post-demonetization." *Forbes*. July 29, 2017.

———. "One Month In, What's the Impact of India's Demonetization Fiasco?" *Forbes*. December 12, 2016.

"Simplifying Life with Easy Finances." Island Pay. n.d. https://islandpay.com /personal.

Singh, Manish. "The Ugly Face of India's Demonetization." Mashable, November 16, 2016. https://mashable.com/article/india-people-dying-demonetization.

Sprenger, Polly. "Sun on Privacy: 'Get Over It." *Wired*. 26 January, 1999. www .wired.com/1999/01/sun-on-privacy-get-over-it.

Summers, Lawrence H. "Accepting the Reality of Secular Stagnation." *Finance & Development*, 57, no. 1 (March 2020). www.elibrary.imf.org/view/journals /022/0057/001/article-A005-en.xml.

———. "The Next President Should Make Infrastructure Spending a Priority." *Washington Post*. September 11, 2016.

Suri, Tavneet. "Mobile Money." *Annual Review of Economics* 9 (2017): 497–520.

Suri, Tavneet, and William Jack. "The Long-Run Poverty and Gender Impacts of Mobile Money." *Science* 354, no. 6317 (2016): 1288–92.

Suri, Tavneet, William Jack, and Thomas M. Stoker. "Documenting the Birth of a Financial Economy." *PNAS* 109, no. 26 (2012): 10257–62.

"The Sveriges Riksbank Prize in Economic Sciences in Memory of Alfred Nobel 2007." Nobel Prize. n.d. www.nobelprize.org/prizes/economic-sciences/2007/summary.

"Swish." n.d. www.swish.nu/about-swish.

"Swiss Bank Pleads Guilty in Manhattan Federal Court to Conspiracy to Evade Taxes." Press release. United States Attorney for the Southern Districts. January 3, 2013. www.justice.gov/usao-sdny/pr/swiss-bank-pleads-guilty-manhattan-federal-court-conspiracy-evade-taxes.

Testimony of Secretary of the Treasury Janet L. Yellen before the Committee on Financial Services, US House of Representatives. May 12, 2022, https:// home.treasury.gov/news/press-releases/jy0776.

US Federal Reserve. *Money and Payments: The U.S. Dollar in the Age of Digital Transformation*. January 2022. www.federalreserve.gov/publications/files /money-and-payments-20220120. pdf.

Van Zuylen-Wood, Simon. "Ian Freeman Could Have Been a Bitcoin Billionaire. Instead He Could Go to Prison for the Rest of His Life." *New York* magazine. August 25, 2021.

Vega, Nicolas. "Warren Buffett wouldn't buy 'all of the bitcoin in the world' for $25: 'It doesn't produce anything.'" May 2, 2022. www.cnbc.com/2022/05/02/warren-buffett-wouldnt-spend-25-on-all-of-the-bitcoin-in-the-world.html.

"Visa Statement on Involvement in the Libra Association." Visa. October 12, 2019.https://usa.visa.com/visa-everywhere/blog/bdp/2019/10/11/visa-update-1570828991831. html.

"Voluntary Disclosure." The Tax Lawyer. n.d. www.thetaxlawyer.com/voluntary-disclosure.

Warmbrodt, Zachary. "Elizabeth Warren's Anti-crypto Crusade Splits the Left."Politico.March15,2022.www.politico.com/news/2022/03/15/democrats-divided-crypto-future-00015804.

Warren, Samuel, and Louis Brandeis. "The Right to Privacy." *Harvard Law Review* 4, no. 5 (1890): 193–220.

Williamson, Oliver E. *Markets and Hierarchies, Analysis and Antitrust Implications: A Study in the Economics of Internal Organization.* New York: Free Press, 1975.

Working Group on E-CNY Research and Development of the People's Bank of China. *Progress of Research and Development of E-CNY in China.* July 2021. www.pbc.gov.cn/en/3688110/3688172/4157443/4293696/2021071614584691871. pdf.

World Bank. *World Development Indicators 2016.* April 20, 2016. https://issuu.com/world.bank.publications/docs/9781464806834? e = 0/35179276.

Yaffe-Bellany, David. "The Coin That Could Wreck Crypto." *New York Times.* June 17, 2022.

Yellen, Janet L. "A Challenging Decade and a Question for the Future." Herbert Stein Memorial Lecture, National Economists Club, Washington, DC, October 20, 2017, www.federalreserve.gov/newsevents/speech/yellen20171020a.htm.

———. "Challenges Confronting Monetary Policy." Speech at National Association for Business Economics Policy Conference, Washington, DC, March 4, 2013. www.federalreserve.gov/newsevents/speech/yellen20130302a.htm.

———. "Housing Bubbles and Monetary Policy." Speech at the Fourth Annual Haas Gala, San Francisco, CA, October 21, 2005. www.frbsf.org/our-district/press/presidents-speeches/yellen-speeches/2005/october/housing-bubbles-and-monetary-policy.

———. "Remarks from Secretary of the Treasury Janet L. Yellen on Digital Assets." Speech at American University Kogod School of Business Center for Innovation, April 7, 2022, https://home.treasury.gov/news/press-releases /jy0706.

"Yellen Sounds Warning about 'Extremely Inefficient' Bitcoin." CNBC. February 22, 2021. www.cnbc.com/2021/02/22/yellen-sounds-warning-about-extremely-inefficient-bitcoin.html.

Zhong, Raymond. "Australia Bars China's Huawei From Building 5G Wireless Network." *New York Times*. August 23, 2018.

———. "In Halting Ant's I.P.O., China Sends a Warning to Business." *New York Times*. November 6, 2020.

Index

deposit insurance, 36

diem. *See* libra/diem model

digital asset policy, 64

digital currencies, private: anonymity of, 80; Buterin and, xi; Chinese e-CNY trial, 119–20, 121–26, 180n32; conditions for, 67–74; as dominant means of exchange, 58, 149–50, 155; fedcoin and, 125–26; global reserve currency and, 12–13, 58; global South and, 45; illicit activity and, 76–77; libra/diem model, ix–xi, 12, 13, 41, 60–65, 67, 84, 149–51; modern payment systems and, 41; network externalities and, x, 10, 12; vs. public digital currencies, 104–5; reputation importance and, 70–71, 149

Digital Currency Research Institute (DCRI), 119, 120

digital payment systems: convenience and security of, 13–14, 18, 19, 22, 165n5; coordination game and, 27–28; digital vs. mobile money, 44–45, 85–86, 118–19; dominant medium of exchange and, 59–60; financial inclusivity of, 23; global reserve currency and, 109; lack of anonymity and, xii, 22; private Chinese mobile money, 118–19, 121, 122–24, 181n37; reduced transaction costs by, 17; smartphones and, 3, 4, 11, 23, 24; transactions overview, 40–41

discount window, 38

distributed-ledger technology (DLT), 7–8, 9–10, 12, 13, 87, 93, 126, 157. *See also* blockchains

diversifying risk, 35

division of labor (production), 1–2

doctrine of monetarism, 99

e-CNY, 119–20, 121–26, 180n27

economic crisis (2008). *See* financial crisis (2008)

economic equilibrium, 155–56

economic realism, 154

Eldredge, Niles, 109–10

Electronic Payments Network, 41, 60

emerging-market economies, xii, 139–41

equilibrium outcomes, 157–58

equilibrium real rate of interest, 100, 127, 129, 131, 132*fig.*

ether (ETH), x, 9, 10, 53, 150

Ethereum, xi, 52–53, 61–62, 82, 91, 155, 173n74

European Central Bank (ECB), 38, 131

exorbitant privilege, 12, 108–9, 110, 112

Facebook: Amazon web services and, 69; Libra Association and, 64–67, 69–70; libra/diem model, ix–xi, 12, 13, 41, 60–65, 67, 84, 149–51; mobile money and, 45; network externalities and, 58; reputation and, 70–71, 149; share structure of, 11; startup capital investment and, 5, 130

fedcoin: acceptance of, 158–59; CBDC models and, 12–13, 27, 72, 85–93, 97–98, 99, 103–6; central banker toolkit and, 99–101; centralized ledgers and, 89–90, 92, 93–94, 97, 126, 156; current monetary policy and, 97–99; customer competition and, 90–91; equilibrium outcomes and, 157–58; financial inclusion and, 151; functional competi-

About the Author

Richard Holden is professor of economics at UNSW Sydney, a fellow of the Econometric Society, and a fellow and president of the Academy of the Social Sciences in Australia. He was previously on the faculty at the University of Chicago and MIT and holds a PhD in economics from Harvard University. He is the author, most recently, of *From Free to Fair Markets: Liberalism after COVID-19*, with Rosalind Dixon.

Founded in 1893,
UNIVERSITY OF CALIFORNIA PRESS
publishes bold, progressive books and journals
on topics in the arts, humanities, social sciences,
and natural sciences—with a focus on social
justice issues—that inspire thought and action
among readers worldwide.

The UC PRESS FOUNDATION
raises funds to uphold the press's vital role
as an independent, nonprofit publisher, and
receives philanthropic support from a wide
range of individuals and institutions—and from
committed readers like you. To learn more, visit
ucpress.edu/supportus.